THE BUSINESS OF BEING PSYCHIC

by Viola

THE BUSINESS OF BEING PSYCHIC

TABLE OF CONTENTS

PREFACE

Hello Reader—you being the reader of this book, and the you who also does psychic readings!

Let me start by saying that this book isn't meant to teach you how to do psychic readings, nor is it meant to teach you how to be psychic. What it *is* meant to do is to identify and define all of the components required in order to be a professional psychic, and then to lead you to conclude for yourself whether or not you could—or even should—be a professional psychic. If you conclude that you indeed could and should, I offer guidance on how to be a psychic in business—more specifically, how to be a successful and profitable psychic. For those of you who already have a gainful practice, I suggest additional ways for you to take your business to the next level and become an even more successful and profitable psychic.

This book is a product of my unsatisfying search for practical professional advice for a spiritually-based business. I had a hard time finding a comprehensive guide for the budding psychic who was trying to determine whether or not they're up to the task of being a professional psychic, and if they were, how and where to begin establishing themselves as such. I was also hard-pressed to find any real applicable, meaty, pertinent-to-psychics business advice for those already in an established practice, but who wished to expand their practice, their clientele, as well as their incomes.

Moreover, I recognized the need for a source of guiding principles that would dissuade someone who shouldn't be a professional psychic from trying to be one—and there is a definite need for that. There are individuals who need to, ever so gently (maybe not so gently in some cases), be dissuaded from doing this work. I bet most of us have had a reading where we wished that the person who gave us the reading had been the recipient of some dissuasion! Am I right?! So, another objective of this book is to discourage psychic pedestrians from setting up shop. It's a dirty job but somebody's gotta do it, and I'm doing it to guard the reputations of, not only creditable intuitive counselors, but also of the intuitive counseling profession itself.

The old adage of *one bad apple can spoil the whole bunch* is relevant here, in that the words and actions of a bad psychic can tarnish this profession as a whole. For instance, if someone has never had a reading before and their first experience is with a reader whose demeanor is harsh, judgmental, or disrespectful, there's the possibility that they'll think that all readers are like that—and if the reader is inaccurate to boot, in all likelihood, that will be their last experience consulting with any "so-called" psychic. An even worse scenario is if someone gets duped by a Madam I'll-Take-The-Curse-Off-You-For-A-Thousand-Dollars. The thing is, that duped person could've been your client or mine, but after an experience like either of those, it's easy to see how they'd lump us all into the same category of fakes, freaks, charlatans (and some other not so polite terms).

Another consequence of someone's negative experience at the hands of a bad reader is that that individual won't ever seek out and benefit from the kind of spiritual guidance that can only come from a good and masterful intuitive counselor.

Developing psychic ability is easy. From reading a book or two it's possible for anyone to discover and start using their psychic abilities. If one would rather take classes, a myriad is offered in many different venues, i.e., metaphysical shops, online, DVDs, from other psychics, etc. It's not hard to find instruction on how to read tarot cards, use a pendulum, dialogue with the dead, or whatever psychic vehicle is preferred. Unfortunately, though, in most books and workshops, the client counseling aspects of the work are all but neglected. Don't get me wrong, I say amen to psychic development. But what happens then is that some very well-intentioned individuals believe that just because they've read the book, took the class, or now know their spirit guide's name, that they're capable of doing readings for the masses. To that I say, **"NO, NO, NO, DEAR GOD, NO!!"** That's not just irresponsible, it's potentially dangerous. Having a little bit of knowledge and then putting that little bit into practice can be a very disastrous formula. I mean, most of us can give heartworm meds to our dogs, and maybe even a vaccination, but it doesn't mean we should be practicing veterinary medicine! Similarly, being psychic and being able to predict a promotion, a marriage, or even a death, isn't enough to be a *practicing* psychic.

So, I won't apologize one iota for asking someone to take a personal inventory, not just of their psychic abilities, but of all the other necessary elements needed for doing this work, such as temperament and conduct, the ability to counsel people in distress, and the skill of working with troubled people.

There's much more to being a practicing psychic than simply using one's sixth sense. There are other important senses required. Some of them can be taught, but not all can be learned. Namely, there's common sense, a sense of responsibility, a sense of boundaries, the sense of what's right and wrong, a sense of humility, being able to make sense, and very importantly, a heck of a good sense of humor. If and when someone has those senses down pat, there's another important sense that would be well worth acquiring by a psychic who wishes to make a living doing this work—a decent living, that is—and that's business sense.

Many psychics have "all the right stuff," and yet they can't seem to make a good enough living to be able to quit their day jobs. What's missing for them is having the benefit of business know-how pertinent to an intuitive counseling practice. I can speak to this first hand. Prior to putting out my "shingle," I thought I'd done enough to prepare myself. After all, I studied under a very gifted psychic, I'd taken a gazillion classes, read innumerable books on anything and everything even remotely related to metaphysics—and I'm a Pisces for God's sake, ya can't be any more sensitive than that! However, when the shingle got put out, I was completely clueless—and it showed. I made every conceivable mistake as a psychic, and even more mistakes as a small business owner. Except for my own inner guidance (and, seriously, how often do we completely listen to our OWN guidance—that's why we go to psychics!), I had nothin' and no one to help me navigate the path.

It was only after writing my first book, *How Not To Do A Psychic Reading* (a book, the revised version, I highly recommend), that a few of my psychic friends shared similar stories of how they, too, had to learn on their own how to create a livelihood using their gifts. The consensus was that if we'd had some practical tutelage or business advice when we were starting out, it would've been a heck of a lot easier! Having some first-hand know-how would've saved us a lot of time, we might've made a better living, and, in many instances, we could've avoided some embarrassment. We all agreed that being psychic was the easy part.

I'm sharing in these pages what I've learned over the years on how to build a good, solid practice, and then grow it even more.

Through trial and many, many errors, I've learned what works. More importantly, I've learned what doesn't work. Everything I relate in this book I've either experienced personally, witnessed firsthand, or had the experience shared with me by a trusted colleague. Mostly, I draw from my own bag of big, fat, ugly faux pas. In the beginning of my career, I very often made a huge ass out of myself (although I probably still do make an ass out of myself from time to time!). My hope is that by my sharing what I've learned, you'll know better and won't make an ass out of yourself—and, in turn, clients won't have to experience the faux pas of big asses!

Surviving my own blunders certainly doesn't make me the supreme authority on psychic professionalism; however, because of those blunders, I know of what I speak. Neither am I claiming be the Ms. Manners of the psychic world or a spiritual hall monitor! Good grief, if anything, I'm more like an Erma Bombeck or the Lucille Ball of the metaphysical world!! My intention is to be the good, albeit blunt, friend that tells you that you have broccoli in your teeth. Or else, the buddy who tells you that you've had too much to drink and hides your cellphone so that you don't call your ex and make a complete ass out of yourself!

I consider this a meeting of the minds with you, the reader. That's why I write in a funnily serious conversational manner. At times, it may seem like I'm being critical, maybe a bit harsh, snarky, possibly even judgmental, but please know that that's not the vein in which I offer this. Although I do admit to uncontrollable sarcasm—but I can't help it, it's just my nature! Mostly, I just call a spade a spade, and that, too, is my nature.

Therefore, incorporate into your business plan whatever suggestion or bit of advice that resonates with you and simply leave the rest. Just like items that are offered at a buffet, you don't have to put it all on your plate, only the things you like.

With that, if you are among the few, the proud, and the psychic, May The Force be with you—and may your business of being psychic prosper!

And now, let's get down to business!

CHAPTER 1:

YOUR CALLING

Wanted: Psychics/Intuitive Readers/Spiritual Counselors. Qualifications required: honesty, integrity, inclusive, proficiency in predicting events, exemplary communication skills with both Source and Earthlings. Must be non-judgmental, compassionate, willing and able to provide comfort, encouragement, and hope, all the while maintaining strong personal boundaries and a sense of humor. A well-kempt appearance is very much appreciated. Narcissists, ego-maniacs, xenophobes, the intolerant, and/or charlatans need not apply. If you are drawn to this ad, inquire within your Self to see if you are qualified. If you are qualified, please respond to this calling.

You won't find a posting like this in your local classifieds or on Monster.com. Oh, you'll find many ads looking for psychics, tarot readers, mediums, and the like, to work on psychic hotlines, or "chat lines," as they're called these days (the longer you keep the client chatting, the more money is made). However, in some of these ads the basic requirements and experience needed can be pretty loose and sketchy. In fact, sometimes the only requirements asked of applicants are that they have a phone and a gift of gab.

Actually, the above is what I imagine a want ad placed by Source would read like. It's my attempt at articulating what I believe the prerequisites are to be a professional psychic—and to have the calling.

The calling comes from deep within. That's how Source calls. By Source, I mean your soul, your Higher Self, God, your Inner Being, Infinite Wisdom, Divine Intelligence, The Voices (by the way, if you call it "The Voices," do be careful who you say that to!), or whatever else you might call it—including It. When you've got the calling to be a professional psychic, it's felt like an urging from the depths of your being to express your psychic gifts and to use those gifts in service to others. But, of course, just like any other job, we can do it half-assed or excel at it.

First, allow me to sidetrack for a moment to avoid any confusion later on. Throughout this book, when I refer to psychics, I'll randomly use the terms "readers," "intuitives," and "spiritual counselors," among others. To me, "psychic" is an umbrella term, and under that umbrella, I include readers of tarot cards, palms, the

I-Ching, tea leaves, crystal balls, mediums, animal communicators, each of the "clairs" (clairvoyants, clairaudients, clairsentients), and so on. Also, I categorize astrologers and numerologists as psychics, although some in the metaphysical world don't agree with that. I beg to differ. More often than not, astrologers and numerologists use their intuition when interpreting—when they "read"—their clients' charts. Furthermore, I refer to energy workers, medical intuitives, and spiritual healers as psychics, as well. After all, they too use psychic abilities to do what they do. The common denominator, whether they're interacting with human beings or with animals, is that they each use their psychic-ness in their own inimitable way. As far as I'm concerned, they all had the calling to do their variation of psychicing, therefore, they're all psychics. By the way, if you're questioning whether or not "psychic-ing" is a word, let me assure you that if you have the calling, psychicing isn't only a word, it's also a way of life!

Now, to be a professional psychic or not to be a professional psychic, that is the question. It's not a question that's posed to everyone, only to the few to whom it's absolutely, positively, crystal-clear that they have the calling. I would venture to say that for most individuals who have psychic abilities, there'll be no calling to be found. Being psychic isn't qualification enough to work with people who bring their challenges, their crises, and the ruins of their lives into the reading room. Other crucial skills are needed.

Without question, it's essential for a professional psychic to have people skills. Or, as I like to say, they've got to have a good "table-side" manner. This is, after all, a people business, so it helps if one is a bit of a people person and is somewhat skilled in dealing with people—all kinds of people in all different situations. Without that ability, one is a misfit, and that's not meant as a derogatory statement.

Needless to say, every occupation has its share of misfits, meaning that there are people in jobs for which they're not ideally suited. Thus, they're an improper fit—or, a mis-fit. If I had to give this "condition" a clinical term, I'd call it the Square-Peg-Trying-To-Fit-Into-A-Round-Hole-Syndrome, heretofore, SPTTFIARHS. It's easy to spot people who are afflicted with SPTTFIARHS, as they're the ones that force themselves into career situations that don't resonate with their core being, that don't make them happy, and makes the people they work with say, *geez, ol' so-and-so has SPTTFIARH*! Yet, they try to make the career fit—and always for all the wrong reasons. Oftentimes, they're just going where the money is. Otherwise, it's the lure of the power and sex appeal that they find attractive that goes along with a particular profession, like say, being on the Geek Squad. Or else, it's one that's fashionable at the moment. Perhaps a reality show star or President of the United States (which can be one in the same)? By far, the worst reason of all that some folks force-fit a profession is because of the influence (a.k.a., control) of other people in their lives.

The good news is that SPTTFIARHS doesn't have to be terminal because there's a cure for it. It's called self-awareness. The remedy requires one to heed one's calling, and then actively pursue the change to what *is* a perfect fit for their square-peg self. On the other hand, if they resist and plod along in unawareness, they just continue to be unhappy campers—and, oh joy, they just keep spreading their unhappiness with the world.

To illustrate, let me use an analogy of a doctor, because I just love to pick on doctors (if something feels good, do it!). So, there's a doctor who's brilliant in her particular field of medicine; of which she's unsurpassed in her theoretical and technical knowledge. Nonetheless, this doctor has zero capacity for empathy and has the personality of Dr. Spock (of Star Trek fame, not the child-rearing guy)—definitely not what you'd call warm and fuzzy. It's no surprise then that her patients dread meeting with her more than they dread a bad diagnosis. Still, she insists on meeting with patients face-to-face. It would be fair to say that this doctor had no self-awareness, wouldn't you agree? If she had even half a clue, she'd recognize that having any direct contact with a conscious patient is not her calling. If she were in touch with her Higher Wisdom, she'd realize that her talents would be best employed elsewhere, such as in research, lecturing, writing, surgery (because those patients are anesthetized!), or in some other form of non-contact medical practice.

When it comes to a career, as well as our place in the world, self-awareness is paramount. Self-awareness is an absolute must if you're going to even entertain the idea of becoming a professional psychic. Your abilities have to go beyond just being able to read some cards, see some dead people, find lost objects, or talk to someone's Nana. It takes a multi-faceted personality, one that possesses basic inherent traits, like kindness and understanding, along with keen human relations skills. It necessitates knowing when to be gentle and when to practice tough love. It demands complete awareness of your own limitations, as well as the limitations of those you're working with. And it requires the ability to accept those limitations gracefully, especially your own. A prerequisite to doing this work—and doing it well—is to have an awareness of human nature, which means having an acute awareness of your own nature (assuming that you're human). Above all, you need a resolute and intimate awareness of your connection to Source. Only then will you know whether you're truly called to do this work—or not.

As I've said, being psychic doesn't mean one is called, because fundamentally, we're all psychic, and everyone has some degree of intuitiveness. It's called many things, such as, "a woman's intuition (sorry gentlemen)," "a knowing," "second sight," and of course, our "sixth sense." I, however, like to call it our psychicness. Some folks possess a higher degree of psychicness than others—like psychics, for instance! And the more someone uses their psychicness, the stronger it gets.

The average person uses their psychicness all the time, even though they don't know they're using it, and they probably don't call it that. For instance, a person will say that they got a gut feeling, had a hunch, or that they didn't get a good "vibe" about someone or something. In fact, what they're doing is picking up on the energy. That's being psychic.

One of the first lessons taught in self-defense courses is to pay close attention to your environment and to get a "feel" for your surroundings. What the instructors particularly emphasize for people to do is to always trust that feeling of when the hairs on the back of their neck stand up. That's feeling the vibes. That's being psychic. Empathy is another form of psychicness. Like when a man feels his pregnant wife's discomfort or cravings, or when he experiences sympathy labor pains, he's being empathetic. He's being psychic.

Those are just a few examples of how we're all psychic to some degree or another. But not everyone who gets a feeling, has a hunch, or has a craving for ice cream and pickles should be in practice as a professional psychic. To repeat, just because a person *is* psychic, doesn't mean they should *be* a psychic. There's much more that goes along with the "being" part of it.

One of the most foundational components of being a professional psychic is being involved with another human being in a very personal way about their most personal matters. We, as the psychics, are being invited into an individual's most trusted circle of confidantes. Hell, sometimes the psychic is a client's *only* confidante. And in that role, we're not only privy to the details of the client's current life, but potentially to their past and future lives, as well. We're also granted access to the workings, or non-workings, of the client's physical body, to the layers of their energy bodies, to what's happening in their subconscious mind, to the person's Akashic records, and more. This access isn't something to be taken lightly, contrary to the disclaimers posted by psychic hotlines or in front of the fortune teller's tent at the carnival! Folks, this is NOT for entertainment purposes only!!

On the contrary, this is some real serious stuff. And those that receive the calling know that. That's why some of them make a conscious choice not to jump to answer the call. These intuitives *intuitively* know what a great responsibility it is to do this work. So, they resist it by either pretending not to hear the calling or by drowning it out with chaos of one kind or another. Feigning deafness or dumbness to the call can work for a time, but it's always gonna be stirring in the background.

If you're in sync with your Inner Being, those stirrings come softly and gently, as a knowingness. But when you're not so in sync, or you're cluttering the channel with energetic debris, it may take a while, but eventually it'll be like a bullhorn in your ear or a two-by-four upside the head! Of course, you can't fault anyone but yourself for that—after all, you signed up for this gig before coming here, thus, your Higher Self is only lending a hand to remind you of that! Of course, you always have a choice, in that you can listen the easy way or you can listen the hard way, because, have no doubt, The Universe has ways of getting our attention. The Bible is full of attention-getters—dare I say that they were of biblical proportion?! There was the burning bush, people being turned into pillars of salt, the various and sundry floods, swarms of locusts, and plagues. And who can forget the killing of all the first-borns in Egypt? Sounds like bullhorns and two-by-fours to me! Oh, those were the days......

Hopefully you didn't need to be hit with a two-by-four or be swarmed by locusts to hear your calling, but for some of the more thick-headed among us, that's what it takes. If we're heading down some metaphorical dark roads and ignoring our Guidance, we'll co-create with the Universe some attention-getter like an illness, an accident, or another kind of crisis. In my case, it was being hit by a car. It's an understatement to say that I wasn't going in the direction I signed on for. But when I became a drunk-driver's hood ornament, I got the message loud and clear! Therefore, from personal experience, I suggest going the route of following the gentle, soft stirrings that come from Within!

Until the adults in their life talk them out of it, children tend to know early on what their purpose is. We hear it all the time from public figures who tell their stories of how they "knew" as children what they were called to do. For instance:

- The budding actors would dress up and put on shows for their families.
- The little musicians would beat on pots and pans because they had the music in them—much to the delight of their parents (and neighbors, I'm sure!).
- The blossoming artist would have a Crayola in each hand always looking for blank wall space to embellish.
- The miniature politician would talk incessantly and make all kinds of promises they wouldn't keep......

I bet even rodeo clowns are called to their specialty. I can just imagine that as children they donned neon wigs and big, red, bulbous rubber noses and hopped around and danced in front of livestock. Or, if they happened to be a city kid, they dodged in and out of traffic. Well, hopefully they dodged the traffic. So, maybe it's actually head injuries that cause these kids to want to piss off already pissed off bulls. Okay then, forget that, rodeo clowns are not a good example. Anyway......

Then there are children who "know" that they are destined for spiritual work. Unfortunately, public schools still only teach reading, writing, arithmetic—and the reading part only pertains to written language, not intuitive counseling! But imagine this scenario:

It's the first day of school and the teacher wants to get to know his bright new second grade students. He goes around the room asking each child the question, "What do you want to be when you grow up?" He asks Ronnie, who replies, "I want to be a veterinarian and help animals get better when they're sick." "Oh, how wonderful!" says the teacher. The teacher then asks Colleen, who answers, "I want to be a police officer and help protect people and keep them safe." "How noble and brave!" says the teacher.

Then, he asks Rose what she wants to be when she grows up. Rose stands up and proudly announces to the class, "I want to be a psychic and tell people what's going to happen to them and talk to the people that've died in their family." Holy crap! Unless the teacher is a New Agey, he'll pick his jaw up off the floor and yank poor Rose off to the principal's office! Then, unless the principal is an enlightened being, it's immediately off to the nurse's office for little Rose!! Her parents would be called in to come and get her and they'd be advised to put her on medication.

And, good grief, we all know how kids can be—who the hell would want to be Rose on the playground at recess after that?!

Perhaps you had an inkling of your calling when you were a child. If you did, I hope you were fully supported—and not put on meds! Also, I hope you were encouraged to listen to The Voices. And with all my heart I hope that you weren't mocked or berated.

I had a negative experience when I was a kid where a teacher made me feel like a freak of nature. As I recall, it was probably either the fifth or sixth grade, and our assignment was to read a book on a subject—any subject at all, mind you— that we had a particular interest in, and then write a book report on it. Well, I was really fascinated by the Salem witch trials (past life memory perhaps?), so I found a book on it and wrote my report. When it came time to get our graded papers back, the teacher sternly called me up to her desk and held up my report. It had a huge "D" on it. While still holding it, she said, very loudly for all the class to hear, something like, *this is not nice, it's evil, and you shouldn't be reading things like this.* I couldn't have felt more ashamed. It wasn't until I got home that I took a look at my report and I found that the teacher didn't make a lot of corrections with respect to my grammar or use of punctuation. Instead, her issue was with the subject matter.

But that was a very long time ago. Being the highly evolved person I am today, and having the great depth of understanding of people that I do, when I think back to that event all those years ago, all I can say is, *I bet that bitch had me burned at the stake back in Salem, so in this incarnation, I hope she burned up in menopause!!!* Oh yeah, and I forgive her.

Heeding the call and making the conscious decision to step into being a professional psychic takes more than just a little bit of courage. To say that pursuing a career as a psychic is unconventional, non-traditional, and non-mainstream, is an understatement (ya think?!). But times are a'changin' and so is the way psychics are perceived. Part of that change can be attributed to a number of television shows that have depicted psychics as everyday folks, albeit not necessarily in everyday situations. They demonstrate that psychics aren't freaks of nature and that the paranormal itself needn't be feared. Still, spiritual practitioners are pretty much viewed as a weird monolithic lot. Believe it or not, there are still people whose only exposure to a psychic has been the Reverend Gonna-Tell-Your-Fortune, complete with a big neon hand in her window! Needless to say, the profession needs an image makeover!

The makeover can't happen quickly enough. More than ever before, there's a great need in our world for spiritual guidance. People are being blasted twenty-four hours a day, seven days a week, with shock wave after shock wave of images that assault the senses, a.k.a., the news. It's a constant bombardment of fear-inducing messages: wars, terrorism, mass-shootings, pandemics, cataclysmic weather, economic collapse, the Kardashians, a vagina-grabbing, porn-star banging, American president, etc., etc. Even those of us who make a concerted effort to avoid the bombardment can't help but be hit with the of-the-moment evil and whatever awful is happening. All it takes is logging onto the internet, and boom, want it or not, death and destruction before your eyes! What's crazier is that there are people who actually sign up to have the most current doom and gloom updates sent directly to their phones—then they wonder why they can't sleep at night and why they live in fear and dread. Duh!

But God love 'em and we should too. I mean, talk about job creation! The masses are seeking help in trying to find clarity in a world that seems unclear to them. They're seeking help in trying to find hope for the future that they view as bleak. They're seeking help in trying to be optimistic when optimism is the last thing they feel. What they seek most, and most of them don't know it's what they most seek, is help in remembering who they really are. That's where we come in. We can be that help they've been seeking. That's why we're called.

If you think that sounds like heavy stuff, you're right, it is. That's why we don't choose this profession. It chooses us. Your choice is whether or not to answer the calling. And if you answer "yes," you can, hand-in-hand with Infinite Intelligence, be of great service to many people and make a difference in many lives.

Now, back to the ad that this chapter began with. Do you believe that you're someone who's qualified to apply for that position? You'll know for sure whether or not you are if you take the quiet time and space necessary to "inquire Within." Block your Ego, get out of your conscious mind, assess your personality, and listen closely to your Inner Being. If you have the knowingness that you're being called to do this work—and trust me, it is, without question, a lot of work—I truly hope you heed that call. If you are indeed being called, you aren't just wanted, you are needed.

With that, let me be kinda-sorta profound and original:

Now is the time for all good psychics to come to the aid of their planet.

And you may quote me!

*

In the business of being psychic, if you have all the right stuff, and you know you're being called, then heed your calling post haste. Believe in your Self, believe in your Source, and let your Light Self shine! Answer your calling with all six senses wide open!

CHAPTER 2:

YOUR PSYCHICNESS

Psychicness is an innate ability that every living creature on this planet possesses. It's one of our senses (ranked sixth, but personally, I rank it much higher). As I said in the previous chapter, everyone is psychic to some extent or another, but what varies from person to person is the degree of their psychicness. And the variance is owing to how much they listen to it—or choose not to. Our psychic muscles work no different than the muscles in our physical bodies. When we exercise them regularly and if we strength-train them, the stronger they become and the more we can depend on them. If we don't use them, just like our physical muscles, they'll atrophy.

Your psychicness is inherently and inimitably yours, so how you tap into it is completely irrelevant. How you channel guidance for your clientele doesn't matter one itty-bitty bit. What is relevant is that your psychicness provides your clients with good, accurate, and helpful information. What also matters is that the information comes from where it should be coming from: Source, Spirit, God, Higher Consciousness, Infinite Intelligence, or you name it. Seriously, just name it and call it that!

Psychicness comes in all ways and means. You might be any of the "clairs": clairvoyant, clairaudient, clairsentient. Or maybe your modus operandi is that you lay down cards, you stare into a cup of tea leaves, you swing a pendulum, or you gaze into a crystal ball (talk about perpetuating the stereotype!). Then again, perhaps you stare off into space and just let things flow to you and through you. However you channel your psychicness is insignificant to your clients, just so long as you can deliver the goods to them.

I'm stressing this point—and getting up on my little soapbox—about psychic individuality because of disparaging things I've come across in promotional materials. In the advertising literature of more than a few psychics, I've found that they're promoting themselves at the expense of demoting other psychics. Instead of advancing their own abilities and standing on their own merits, they disparage other psychics in one way or another. And this is in a profession that's supposed to be based on tapping into Universal Love! That kind of crap is anything but Universal Love!!

Not long ago, I ran across a particular psychic's website and was completely put off by what I read. I will name no names or websites because I'm trying to practice that Universal Love stuff and all…. In it, they made a point of belittling other psychics for "using" something to do readings with, such as cards, runes, a pendulum, etc. The dialogue went on to say that those who had to utilize a tool weren't "pure" psychics. Well, I say hogwash to that! If a psychic doesn't need a tool or a vehicle to work with, more power to them, but I don't believe it makes them any more "pure," and it certainly doesn't make them a better psychic. Many absolutely phenomenal psychics will use a tool, whether it's to tune in, to bring in more detail to the reading, or to verify the information that comes through. Using a tool is simply a means by which to focus, but by no means does it make a reader less psychic or diminish their psychicness.

Tarot card readers particularly are haunted by that judgement. There's always been some debate in the metaphysical world about whether or not tarot card readers should be considered psychics. It's true that most classic tarot readers do, in fact, strictly interpret the meaning of the cards, and the placement of those cards within the spread, but more often than not, tarot card readers read intuitively. They'll receive feelings, impressions, and messages that aren't on any of the cards. Essentially, they utilize their psychicness while interpreting the cards. In my book, that legitimizes their psychicness.

As I mentioned previously, astrologers and numerologists aren't generally categorized as psychics. I see that differently. They, indeed, do their forecasting by employing astrology or numerology; however, many of them will tell you that they "sit" with the client's charts and "tune in" and get a "feel" for how the planets or numbers have influenced, and will be influencing, the client. They use their psychicness.

Whether you use a tool or not, and regardless of what "they" say, if you've answered your calling and are using your psychicness for the greater good, you're unquestionably a psychic! And, I might add, much more "pure" than one who suffers delusions of grandeur. Okay, I'm off my soapbox now and back to your psychicness.

If your intention is to be a professional psychic, if you're going to use your psychicness to make your living, the degree of your psychicness should be superior to the average person. A good example is the difference between someone who goes out for an occasional stroll around the block and someone who's an elite marathon runner. If you were taking up running, who would you ask to coach you? Being a professional psychic requires the extrasensory to be extra-ordinary. That means that before you turn pro, you need to honestly and objectively gauge your abilities.

However, first let's look at what can make your psychicness appear totally moot, and that would be what I call "the variables" (frankly, I call them the f*@#ing variables, but that's only when they've made *my* psychicness look moot). The variables are the choices, decisions, contradictions, and actions your clients make—or don't make—after a reading. When you're assessing your psychicness, you'll have to allow that variables can (and will) alter—or completely negate—any insights you get and any predictions you make. What's especially important to keep in mind about variables is that you have absolutely no control over them. Actually, in this work—just as in life overall—recognizing right from the get-go that you have no control over anything (except your own thoughts) will keep you sane—unless you're a control-is-how-you-roll Virgo, Capricorn, or Scorpio!

So now let me illustrate how variables can throw a wrench into your perfectly accurate prediction—and, thus, your client deems your psychicness *wrong*:

- A client snarkily reports to you that he didn't get the promotion you predicted he'd get. What he neglects to tell you is that he got more than a little cocky around the office and he started slacking off at work. The variables are the cocky and the slacking. But *you* will be called wrong because, after all, *you said*.

- Your crushed client tells you that her boyfriend didn't propose on Valentine's Day like you predicted. However, she doesn't tell you that she dragged him to a high-end jewelry store and told him exactly which ring he **will** buy, then shoved a calendar under his face telling him to pick a date for a wedding, effectively scaring any proposal (and everything in his intestines) out of him. The technical term for that variable is, I believe, bossy bitch. But it will be *you* that will be wrong because, after all, *you said*.

- A completely perplexed client lumbers in and tells you that she didn't lose the weight that you predicted she would. What she omits to tell you is that after the reading she stopped eating healthy foods and quit exercising. Even worse, she allowed her sweet tooth again to run rampant. Clearly, there are several variables at work here: addiction, self-sabotage, lack of self-esteem, just to name the obvious ones. But it will be *you* that was wrong because, after all, *you said*.

Et cetera, et cetera, et cetera, ad nauseam.

Predictions by the best psychics in the world aren't immune to being thwarted by a client's contradictions about their desires. In those cases, it's not about the psychic's psychicness malfunctioning; it's about the contrariness of the client. A person has to be ready, or at least be willing to be ready, on all levels—mentally, emotionally, physically, subconsciously—for what they think they want and what they're asking for to manifest. If they're not ready and open, the person, place, thing, or whatever they think they desire, either doesn't manifest at all, or else it does show up for them but then they refuse it. Worst case scenario is that they get their desired "it" and then quickly lose it, as in the cases of many lottery jackpot winners.

You'll have many clients swear to you that they want something so desperately that they'd give anything to have it. It might be a better job, a bigger, more beautiful house, a healthier body, a new lover, a Porsche Boxster (yes, *anything,* I say!), or whatever else happens to be their current heart's desire. Your psychicness may see it, your psychicness can just about touch it for them (watch yourself with that regarding the new lover!), but if they have blocks to letting that desire become theirs, you're the only one that will know it's really there. Any of their unresolved issues, like lack of self-esteem, lack of self-worth, issues with their mothers (it's *always* the mother!), or a horde of any other subconscious or energetic issues, can block what they're asking for from coming to them.

At other times your psychicness will predict that their desire is imminent—and then, *VOILA*, just like you said, there it is. But when it shows up for them, just like *you said*, they say (consciously or subconsciously), *"naa, I'll pass."* The reason for the *"naa, I'll pass"* could well be their issue of feeling like they don't deserve what's being offered to them. Or they're just lazy. It's not unusual for someone to decide that what they swore up and down that they wanted is just too much trouble. The better job might be more responsibility and would require more of their time, which would mean less television or beers and bowling with the gang after work. The new bigger house might be breathtakingly beautiful, but that will mean more upkeep and a lot more cleaning involved. A healthier body is going to mean working out for crying out loud and eating stuff that grows in the earth or on trees! The cost of maintenance, tires, and premium gas for the Porsche is outrageous (*I don't care*!). And, of course, we all know how much time, energy, and new underwear a new lover demands.

Here's how the variable of client contrariness can play out:

Let's say you do a reading for a Mr. Wishie Washie and your psychicness sees a most fantastically amazing job opportunity falling into Wishie's lap. (You're on a first-name basis with him because he's a regular of yours, and he's a regular because he can't make up his mind whether or not to consult with another psychic.) On hearing your prediction for him, he's ecstatic! He says that it's been his burning desire for a most fantastically amazing job opportunity to fall into his lap. However, after the reading, and after thinking about this job actually becoming a reality for him, he's undecided about whether he's ready or willing to jump on that opportunity. Mr. Wishie Washie is then sending out mixed signals to the Universe, so, effectively, it's not gonna happen. His change of mind will either create a block causing the job to fall into someone else's lap, or it's offered to him and he declines it, or else he takes it and then promptly gets canned because he doesn't do the job well. Hence, although your brilliant psychicness saw it as a sure thing, it doesn't become his reality.

Among all the many variables, one that is the most powerfully blocking is a lack of belief. I daresay that that's the primary reason why some predictions don't come to fruition. People simply don't believe they can. Your psychicness may tell them that something wonderful is right over the horizon, but if they don't believe it's possible, that can prevent it from manifesting into their current reality. I'm sorry to have to tell you this but your psychicness doesn't stand a chance against someone's lack of belief. Don't *believe* me? Well, then, allow me to demonstrate. Let's pretend you just came to see me for a reading:

Welcome, You, *have a seat, please. Ready? Here we go*:

"Holy crap, this is soooo fabulous! I see you becoming an extraordinarily successful and sought-after psychic! I see you getting your own television show, as well as writing a best-selling book......yep, it's definitely a New York Times best-seller!! I also see you traveling and lecturing around the world. I'm so excited for you! It's a dream come true!! Oh, oh, oh, and this is the best part, I see you making millions and millions of dollars!!!! WOW!!!!"

Would you believe it if that's what I told you? *Could* you believe it? Probably not. Would you allow yourself to even entertain the thought that just possibly, perhaps, maybe, perchance, you could let yourself believe that? In all likelihood, you'd think that I was some lying charlatan carnival sideshow—and you probably wouldn't pay me either!! Predictions like that sound far too fantastical. Most likely your thought would be that (besides that I was a lying charlatan carnival sideshow) it sounds like a dream come true alright—but somebody else's dream!

Honestly, I've never gotten a message like that for anyone, and I know it seems to be an absurd example. But what if you got a reading from another psychic that you trusted, and you knew unequivocally that they wouldn't hand you a load of b.s.? What if they told you that all that good stuff was in your energy field just waiting for you to let it in? Could you, would you, believe it? You probably couldn't believe it, and because you couldn't believe it, it wouldn't actualize. I completely understand that. After all, I don't have a Porsche Boxster yet!

On the other hand, if every fiber of your being believed it, could feel it, just knew it was possible, and expected it, it WOULD happen. It would show up and affirm my psychicness, or that of your trusted psychic-friend. I would hope at that point you'd consider paying me for the reading......and maybe tip me.......since you *are* a celebrity psychic and best-selling author!

It's the belief that it can't happen—and that it certainly can't happen for any of *us*—that so many dreams don't come true and so many predictions don't come to pass. It's sad, really, that most people can't imagine life even slightly improved for themselves, let alone greatly improved. For a psychic, it's frustrating to see something wonderful awaiting a client, predict the something wonderful, then be called "wrong" because the client couldn't see it for themselves, and thus, not allow it to manifest into their present reality. Knowing this probably won't make you feel any better, but that's why some of your predictions won't come to fruition on this plane of existence. It's not an excuse, rather it's a bigger than life variable.

Some variables will seem pretty minor, like someone not getting or taking a new job. Others are more—and literally—life and death. For instance, your psychicness may assure a client that her mother will recover from a stroke and will go home. That may very well be Mom's plan, too. Until, however, Dad (who's already on the other side), makes an appearance, and, hubba hubba, looks like a young stud again, showing Mom what's she's been missing. As you're doing the reading, Mom's telling Hot Papa that she has to stay on the Earth plane because the kids still need her, and now there are the grandchildren, and the birds and the squirrels in the backyard depend on her to feed them, and this, that, and the other. She promises to join him soon, though. And that's the plan as the reading wraps up.

But all that changes as Hot Papa gives his Momma Mia *the look*. She could never resist *the look*. So, she weighs her options. She could stay in the old dehydrated body that is now paralyzed on one side; she could speak in slurs, drool, and rely on people to come in to bathe and dress her—and change her diaper. She could worry that the birds and squirrels aren't being fed. Or else......

Mom chooses *the look* and makes her transition. She utilizes the variable of her free will (I'm with Mom!). But what would that say about your prediction? Well, technically, Mom *did* recover when she went into non-physical, and did, indeed, go "home." It just wasn't home on this physical plane like your client was hoping for, so your client will say that you were wrong.

Another possibility is that you tapped into what is transpiring in a parallel life where Mom stays in her dilapidated body and goes back to her physical residence. If you delve further into that life you would probably see where Mom was really pissed off that she didn't cross over when she had the chance. Her kids—especially your client, the doting daughter—are speaking to her TOO LOUDLY and over-enunciating their words. Mom thinks, *what's wrong with those idiots? Don't they realize that I'm only having problems with my own speech? I'm not deaf or stupid!* Also, the grandkids don't come around, and when they do they seem to be afraid of her. And after a few days of her being gone the birds and squirrels went off and found another food source. What's more, adding insult to all that injury, she's pooping in a diaper instead of doing the Cha-Cha with Hot Papa!

But that sounds like you're trying to cover your ass, so I'd suggest you don't tell your client any of that.

Variables happen. The most comforting thing I can offer is to say to just get used to them tarnishing your psychicness every now and then. After all, you can only relay a message, but you can't force an outcome.

Now, moving on to your abilities and how to determine if you have the psychic chops to be a professional.

Notwithstanding the multitude of variables that clients can (and will) draw in, assess your psychicness. Here are three very key questions to ask:

- How accurate are you?
- How specific and detailed is the information you're able to provide in your readings?
- What is your general time frame for your predictions to come to pass?

Accuracy

The accuracy of your psychicness should be measurably above average. If you're just starting out, practice on your friends and family, and ask them to give you honest feedback, the positive and the negative. Getting feedback is by far the best way to gauge your accuracy. People are usually more than happy to rate you. And, bless their little hearts, people are particularly happy to point out when you're wrong! Consequently, put on your tough skin and brace yourself! Human nature being what it is, they sure won't always remember to let you know and/or give you credit when something good and exciting happened just like you said it would, but, man, oh man, you will be told immediately if not sooner when you're wrong! Nevertheless, appreciate any and all feedback for what it is: an invaluable way to improve your psychicness and expand into being a professional psychic. Bruises and all, warranted or not, it's necessary to take the punches. Also, appreciate the side benefit that comes with it, which is building up a thicker skin!

If you're a seasoned psychic who's been psychic-ing for eons, it's still important to keep tabs on the accuracy of your readings. Now and then, ask a client for feedback. I'm not suggesting that everyone you read for should take a survey after their session. Rather, here and there, ask a client to shoot you an email or text letting you know if the job came through or if they got the Porsche. Above all, don't dismiss any negative feedback you might get. Take it all under advisement and see where you might have not gotten it right and, if so, why. You might find that you're throwing in your own variable.

Let's be real, some of us who've been doing this work for a while will sometimes forget to give the client our full attention, unintentionally, of course. We all have those times when we're on auto-pilot and our thoughts go to the phone calls we need to return or we start thinking about what color to paint the kitchen. Or, again since we're being honest, we get bored. Whether it's because our clients are different faces but the same issues, or the same faces with *always* the *same* issues. Of course, in either case, it's The Universe trying to get a message to us through them, but that's a different conversation. Otherwise, it's that we need a change in our life or even our work (yet another conversation). In any of these instances, our accuracy may not be up to par, and a little feedback from a client may just be the wake-up call we need.

Barring any change of mind or faint of heart on the client's part—or letting their ego seize control away from their Higher Power—how does the accuracy of your psychicness stack up? And barring any inattentiveness to your clients, do you maintain your accuracy, or preferably, continually improve it? Regardless of any other factors, your accuracy rate should be exemplary. If you're going to be a professional, a consistent seventy-five to eighty percent, or better, accuracy is reasonable for clients to expect from you. More importantly, it's what you should expect from yourself.

Specificity

How specific can you get using your psychicness? Clients want, and should expect to receive, specific information when they get a reading. That being said, I first need to add that any specifics a client requests from you should be realistic. Asking you to give them the names of the horses that are going to win the trifecta is not realistic. Therefore, it'll help you a lot to recognize when you and your psychicness are being pushed for unrealistic specifics—and, unfortunately, pushing happens. When it does, don't hesitate to push back! Gently and lovingly, of course. Don't be afraid to point out to a client that they are, in fact, being unreasonable in what they're asking you for. Case in point:

> Not long ago I had a client who had just broken up with her man-of-the-moment. She was questioning whether she did the right thing. In the reading, she was assured that severing that relationship was a very good move on her part. She was told that by shutting that door she was allowing someone new and improved to come in. But what was of even greater value to her was that it was a huge step in her personal growth. Then she was warned that the "ex-moment" was going to call again and try to convince her to get back together. It really didn't take a psychic to see that coming; he was a controlling bastard (that's a personal commentary). She asked me several times, "Will I decide to get back together with him?"

Don't get me wrong, I had great compassion for her, and I understand that people are where they are. But, I also have to admit that my thought was, "Are you freakin' kidding me, lady?!" However, I had my professional hat on. I told her that I didn't know what she was going to decide because I was a psychic and not a mind reader. I explained to her about free will and free choice and pointed out that in her reading she was given much insight into the relationship, which she could use to make her decision about this man. Also, I repeated the message from Higher Intelligence that she'd made a good decision to break off that relationship in the first place.   Then I reminded her that she was told there would be someone new coming into her life if she closed the door to the old. I explained that a psychic can see where it looks like the energy is going, but the purpose of the reading was to provide her with the specifics to make her own decisions. Even more, I tried to help her understand that even her spirit guides can't tell her what to decide, because making her decisions isn't what they do; what they do is *guide*. Otherwise, they'd be called "spirit deciders."

To be clear, I'm not mocking this woman in any way. I'm simply sharing this scenario because it illustrates how clients can be unrealistic in what they're asking for from a psychic. This particular client was provided very specific details in her reading with which to make her own decisions. Instead, she tried to pressure me to tell her how she was going to exert her free will. Huh? That's not just unrealistic, it's nonsensical.

Albeit playfully, I do like to mock a certain group of people. It's single people in search of "The One." They can be some of the most relentlessly unrealistic folks! Of course, it's certainly not unreasonable to be asked what "The One" might look like. BUT, what make, model, and year of the vehicle he or she drives isn't just unrealistic, it's ridiculous! You think I jest, but oh no, I jest not! When you do this work long enough, you'll be asked—if not outright pressured—for all kinds of ridiculous specifics!!

In these situations, I find that the best way to respond is to keep it lighthearted and employ humor. If I'm being pressed—or pressured—I'll say something like, "I'm sorry, I'm not at liberty to give you a full name, address, telephone number, and bank account balance." It usually takes a moment or so for it to sink in, but then they typically laugh at themselves—and, thankfully, back off! Though they want help in their search, they sure don't want to look desperate!

By the way, if you're capable of providing the makes, models, and years of vehicles, you'll be in great demand with the singles crowd! In which case, I suggest you charge a little extra!!

All kidding aside (although I wasn't necessarily kidding about charging extra!), specifics are critical to readings. Be honest with your clients—as well as with yourself—about what specifics you're capable of providing and, equally important, what you're not. The more specific the information and messages that you can provide your clientele, the more you will aid them in making the best possible decisions and choices in their life situations. One of the recurrent complaints we hear from people about a reading they've gotten is that the reader was too vague or dealt only in generalities. That's a really legitimate complaint.

Generalities can be expected in the little blips of horoscopes that are featured in magazines, newspapers, or on websites. If I may sidetrack a moment, I have to defend the blips. Even if the publication or website has a good astrologer providing the forecasts, when only a Sun Sign forecast is read, there's no question that it's going to be vague or general. At a minimum, the Ascendant, or Rising Sign, needs to be read in conjunction with the Sun Sign to get a more complete forecast. Still, it'll be a bit generalized. For a personalized, non-vague, non-generalized forecast, a person needs to consult with a good astrologer. So, media horoscopes are the exceptions for vagueness. Readings given by a professional psychic, however, shouldn't be general or vague.

If people wanted vague, they wouldn't venture outside of their own minds! What they want is spiritual perspective and some clear, practical specifics about their circumstances. That's why they make appointments to sit down with the likes of us. Our job is to hone in on the energy of the circumstances that they can't see for themselves. We will have only done our job well when the client walks away from a consultation with ample clarity and insight to make the decisions that need to be made, as well as resolve any challenges they're facing. The specifics you provide will help them to do that.

Essentially, it's up to us to see the proverbial forest from the trees for them. Your psychicness will help them further if you can tell them *specifically* which forest they're heading toward or which one they might get lost in. Moreover, your psychicness should be able to tell them *specifically* which, if any, of the trees are diseased, or if a tree is about to fall on them, or whether they're barking up the wrong tree! Or maybe that they shouldn't "pine" over any particular tree......or that they need to "branch" out in a new and different direction........I'm going out on a "limb" keeping the tree analogy going…..

The point is that clients have a right to expect to be provided with specific details about their specific situations. Otherwise, why the heck pay to see a psychic? Here's what I mean:

> Say someone is job hunting and has all of the feelings that typically accompany a job search: anxiety, frustration, fear, etc. So, to get some insight about their search they decide to see a psychic. If they're told to *hang in there, job offers are coming* it may give them some encouragement, which is nice, but that's of no real benefit to the client. They can get that kind of pep talk from their friends. They didn't have to consult with a psychic for that.
>
> On the other hand, if the reader tells them specifically that there are two job offers coming in approximately three weeks, and then gives them some specific pieces of information about which of the two jobs might be a better fit, now that's of great benefit. Other specifics, such as something about the company, perhaps what side of town the business is on, or maybe that the job is in another town or even out of state. Armed with that, the client would expand their search. Conceivably, a good psychic might be able to perceive a distinctive building feature, like a big fountain or some weird work of art, or even some marked characteristic or idiosyncrasy about the interviewer. Specifics like that make a great reading and serve clients well.

By far, an area that highlights the significance of specific details that psychics are able to provide is in the area of crime—and I'm talking about solving crimes, not committing them! When police departments contract the services of psychics, they expect specifics, often gory ones. These are the kinds of specifics that only a psychic can deliver—or a fly on the wall, but flies can't talk. Details such as something extraordinary about the crime scene, or an unusual or identifiable appearance of the perpetrator(s) or some peculiar physical trait, or perhaps a part of a license plate or vehicle make, model, or color. They're also interested in the psychic's impressions about the perp's mental state and/or the relationship to the victim. Those kinds of specifics give law enforcement another tool, and a unique perspective, in solving crimes. Sometimes it's one of those specifics that *is* the tool for solving the case. It goes without saying that detectives would love to get a name and address of the perp, but I hear most of those psychics are sequestered away by the government for its own crimes…...I mean purposes......it's just what I hear.

I personally have a great deal of admiration for what psychic detectives do. Not many of us have the desire, let alone the guts, for tuning into such heinous scenarios. Kudos and gratitude to those who do.

So, as you can see, being able to provide as many specifics as possible in a reading is critical—to your clients as well as for your success as a professional psychic. To be fair, unless you're a psychic detective, the majority of the readings you do won't be matters of life and death. But know that for your clients that are in really tough situations, it may feel that way.

Timing

Timing is everything. Time is all relative. Everything in its right time. Time is an illusion. There's a time for everything. And yeah, yeah, yeah, yada, yada, yada! We've all heard these old adages, shall I dare say, *time* after *time!* At the very least, they're comforting statements. But don't try using any of them on your clients when they're relying on you to give them a timeframe to work with. Accurate timing is another important element in your psychicness.

Clients don't only seek out psychics to find out what's going to happen in their lives, but also to find out *when* what's going to happen will happen. If you're going to make it as a professional, it's important that what you predict happens sooner or later—rather than never—but it's equally important to be able to offer a good sense of timing of when your predictions will actualize. For many of your clients, to coin another phrase, time is of the essence. Now, no pressure here, but clients tend to have a lot riding on the timeframe you give them, as in the following:

> Mr. Richie Leech is anxiously waiting for his grandfather to die so that he can receive his inheritance. He's racked up thousands in credit card debt and is struggling to make the minimum payments. He seeks out a psychic to get a sense of time about when the old man is going to wink out. If he's

told that it'll be awhile, poor guy will have to cash in a CD to pay the bills. However, if gramps is going to check out posthaste, he's heading over to the Jaguar dealership right after the reading.

So, you can see the importance of the timing you're able to provide, can't you?!

Seriously, though, timing takes on a whole different meaning when a client is hurting, whether it's emotionally, mentally, or physically. People in pain are desperate for some idea as to how long their pain is going to continue. They want some inkling of how long it'll be before they can expect to see some relief, or else prepare themselves for the long-haul. Your psychicness should be able to give them that inkling or preparedness.

Of course, just as all the other aspects of your psychicness can be sapped by the dreaded variables, your timing is not immune. For example, let's say that you do a reading for a client who is awaiting the great job offer. Your psychicness sees that it'll be coming in approximately three weeks. Given that prediction, the guy decides to quit his current job and live off his one-month of savings. But then here come the variables of worry and doubt, and the "what ifs" creep into his head: what if the offer takes longer to come in, what if my friends were right and I'm crazy to think this could come to me, what if my father was right and I'm stupid and will never amount to much, what if that freaky psychic was wrong????!!! Each one of those thoughts can create a block to that great job coming to him in three weeks—or ever.

Or, in the case of a client in physical pain, perhaps in her reading you saw relief coming in about two weeks. Although she leaves hopeful, before long her focus is completely back on her pain. We can't blame her. Pain is painful, after all, and it will keep one's attention. But if she can't redirect her focus away from the pain, relief can't come to her. After all, whatever we keep our attention on, keeps on keeping on.

There's not much we can do about the variables that thwart timing, but we can help enlighten our clients about how they can allow into their experience what they want in the timeframe predicted for them—or not allow it in at all. When I do a reading, I advise my clients that the timeframe I'm getting for them is what it looks like at the present moment. I'll then encourage them to stay focused on what they want, and, without exception, I'll recommend a book or two or three or a dozen. Good books that feed the mind positivity and empowerment are the anti-variables!

Ultimately, being able to provide accurate timing is worth its weight in gold to clients. That will translate into a thriving business for you, making it worth the "time" you put into!

So, as you can see, exemplary accuracy, specificity, and timing are needed for first-rate psychicness. However, there's another element that helps to pull it all together to complete the package, and that's trust. Trust in yourself, trust in your abilities, and of course, trust in your Guidance. You have to trust what you know, trust what you feel, and trust what you know you know and feel. Got that? Basically, what I mean is that you have to learn to trust completely in your psychicness.

One of the best possible ways to learn this trust is to establish and maintain a clear channel of communication with your Guidance. If your initiation into this work was to have other-worldly beings present themselves physically to you speaking distinctly and audibly (and not scare the hell out of you), you're one of the lucky ones. The rest of us had to learn a whole new way of communicating with what/who we couldn't see. It's like learning another language, but without Rosetta Stone or the aid of hand gestures!

Actually, using the word "language" is somewhat deficient when it comes to trying to describe the communication with Source. What's communicated, and how it's communicated, goes beyond words. Indeed, it's more like a transmission of feelings, sounds, smells, symbols, etc. And the transmissions are unique to each one of us. To say that there's a lot to learn is an understatement! Yet, it's not inaccurate to call it a language. After all, there's the language of love, and that's more than words—and much harder to understand! Heck, compared to that, the language with Source is a piece of cake!

Here's an old joke: how do you get into Carnegie Hall? The answer: practice, practice, practice. That's also the answer to perfecting and trusting the communication with Higher Intelligence—and that's no joke. The more we practice, the more fluent we become in that language. The more fluent we become, the more we trust the communication, which ultimately results in better readings. You just have to decide how fluent you wish to be. It's like the difference between going to a foreign country and being satisfied with simply being able to ask where the bathrooms are or deciding that you want to be able to have in-depth conversations with the locals. For that matter, we get to decide how fluent we wish to be even in our primary language. Some of us will look up a word every now and then to improve our vocabulary. Others of us won't. It's not so different when it comes to your communication with Infinite Intelligence. You may not have a dictionary or thesaurus to turn to for meaning, but you do, in fact, have tools. They'd be your feelings, your third-eye, your sixth sense, your pendulum, your tarot cards, what kind of wildlife is showing up, etc.

After working for a while as a team, you and your Guidance will be able to settle on certain words, feelings (emotional and physical), symbols, and whatever else works for you, that you'll be able to use consistently and reliably in readings. Words and feelings are pretty straightforward, but when you're working with symbols, it pays to be absolutely, positively sure of how the symbol is to be used, like whether it's to be taken literally, or how it's to be interpreted for the particular client. Misinterpreting or misjudging a symbol can get one into a little trouble. I know. Allow me to share a just a couple of my own less-than-stellar moments:

- I had a vision of fish and confidently informed my client that her pet fish were very happy with their lives. She said she didn't have any fish. I then told her that she was going to be getting some fish. She countered that she absolutely was not, she had nothing against fish, but she wanted nothing to do with caring for fish or cleaning a fish tank. Still, I was obnoxiously adamant and insisted that she was going to get some fish and that, by God, she was really going to love her fish! We agreed to disagree, and I moved on. It later came up that her daughter was a Pisces. Oops.

- I made a judgment about someone in a client's life and emphatically called his lady friend "two-faced" and "Sybil." My client was appalled because we were talking about a woman he adored more than life itself. When I asked for her birthday I realized that she was a Gemini. And another one bites the dust.

Those were in my early days, and when I think back to those instances I get a vision of another astrological sign. What I see is Sagittarius.......oh, no, actually, it's just the back end of it.

So, a word to the wise, use symbols in conjunction with your psychicness, not in lieu of it, and don't rely solely on them. What the symbols signify should never be held onto too stubbornly. I learned that through bananas. Since this isn't a children's book I can relate this story. Though, let me begin by saying that I pride myself on having very strong boundaries and being able to detach myself from the people I read for. That's because *I am a professional*. In any situation where I believe I might have even the slightest difficulty in being impartial I ask my Guides to take over. In the following situation, I suspected that I might experience a bit of a challenge in detaching myself. Therefore, I did indeed ask my Guides to take over. That being done, I was confident that I was going to be the professional I pride myself on being. Soooo:

A few years ago, there was a gentleman that I had a very serious crush on. The feelings were mutual, and we were disgustingly flirty with one another. When he found out that I was a psychic he wanted to get a reading from me. I said sure, because *I am a professional*. So, at the appointed time, he arrived at my office and I began the reading. But really quickly I realized that any detachment or impartiality were nowhere to be found. Instead, I became a silly, giggly, blushing, high school girl. But *I am a professional* (that's my story and I'm sticking to it), so I plodded along, although the reading was feeling quite off—as was the reader. Besides my giddiness, I seemed to be misinterpreting one of the symbols I normally get. Pretty much from the beginning of the reading and continuously throughout, I kept seeing a banana. *If you're snickering right now, let me say in my defense that whenever I see a banana in a reading it **always, always, ALWAYS** means either: 1. the client has high blood pressure, or; 2. they have a low potassium count.* So, there I was seeing a banana and asking him over and over and over again if he was sure that he didn't have high blood pressure or if he wasn't low in potassium. He answers, over and over and over again, "no" on both counts. All the same, I keep seeing a banana and I just won't shut up about it! Anyway, because

I am a professional (did I mention that?), I insist he keep tabs on both his blood pressure and his potassium level.

After the reading, it's not a stretch to say that I was more than a little bit miffed at my Guides. I asked them, using words I won't repeat here (because *I am a professional),* what that was all about. In response, I very clearly heard, *hehehe!!!* Assholes.

Most days, I'd say that I'm blessed to have a best friend, a sister really. I wasn't feeling so much that way when I shared my harrowing experience with her over dinner that evening. She knew about the dynamic between this gentleman and me, so when I began to tell her about not only seeing a banana but being stuck on the banana and all I could think of was that banana, food projectiled out of her mouth! Dare I say, there were "peals" of laughter? When she came up for air, she pointed out some very obvious, albeit, not obvious to me, symbolism! I needn't say anything further.

Suffice it to say, I learned to tread carefully when interpreting symbolism! I also learned that my Guides can be practical joking assholes!! And although I lost a client that day because my psychicness was off, I have to admit that my Guides saw the happily-ever-after story that *the professional* didn't. That gentleman is now my husband.

Take my word for it, it's important to be aware that the messages you receive aren't always going to be clear and certainly not delivered to you in perfect syntax. But the more you work to improve the communication between you and your Guidance, the better your psychicness will be, which will make for better readings for your clients—and avoid any embarrassment for yourself! Develop your psychicness by developing the relationship between you and your Guide(s). When relating to other humans it's said that familiarity breeds contempt. That's completely the contrary with Higher Intelligence. In this case, familiarity breeds great psychicness.

To grow as a psychic, and in turn, to grow your practice, your psychicness must continue to grow. Know that it'll always be a work in progress, and there's always room for more and better. Your psychicness is a precious gift and should be treated as such. It's a gift to you from Spirit that should be loved and nurtured like you would love and nurture a child. It's something to fully support, meet its needs, encourage its growth, and help it develop to its fullest potential so it can then go off into the world and make a difference in the lives of many.

In the business of being psychic, your psychicness will be one of the biggest factors in your reputation and in the overall success of your practice. Strive to develop it to your fullest potential. It's an undertaking which will seem never-ending—but never-ending is the potential of your psychicness.

CHAPTER 3:

YOUR OBJECTIVITY

Talk to the hand! No, that's not exactly the attitude I'm encouraging, and I'm certainly not suggesting you actually say that—or display that—to your clients, but using that as imagery or as a silent mantra can be helpful to keep your objectivity when working with your clientele.

The sole purpose of getting a reading from a psychic is to get spiritual guidance from Infinite Intelligence. It's not meant to be an opportunity for the client to unload their box of worries and woes at the psychic's feet. Nor is it an occasion to drag the psychic into their life-dramas or syphon off chi, life force energy, from the psychic. Even so, it's incumbent upon the psychic to remain cognizant of their own energy field, knowing where theirs ends and the client's begins, and remain detached emotionally and mentally. That's objectivity.

To maintain your objectivity, invoke the word "THEIR." As in, clients come to you about THEIR situations, clients are seeking advice for THEIR problems, it's THEIR issues to deal with, it's THEIR lives to navigate. With all of THEIR stuff, it's they that need to make THEIR own decisions. It's crucial that you understand—and you make your clients understand—that you're only the intermediary that imparts the guidance from Infinite Intelligence to them. Once they are comforted, warned, or even armed, with THEIR messages, your job is done. Your sole mission is to be the momentary face and voice of Infinite Intelligence. It's not part of your mission to make THEIR life choices for them. If you didn't get my drift in all that, let me drift more bluntly: THEIR shit is THEIR shit. So *there*.

You will serve your clients best when you're solidly in your objectivity and strictly coming from your psychicness, as opposed to interjecting from your compassion, your humanness, or your conscious mind. Maintaining objectivity ensures that you will be an unfiltered conduit for communication between Spirit and your clients. To the best of your ability, you need to be free of your own mental, emotional, or energetic debris. In other words, you and your ego need to be on hiatus. No personal judgments, no personal opinions, no personal criticisms, no personal directives. Nothing personal.

Getting the messages for our clients can sometimes seem like a breeze compared to keeping ourselves in our objectivity. The reason for that is our pesky humanness. (Yeah, you're human, and the sooner you face it, the better—and, by the way, you can't help it, you were born that way!) Like any other human, you have opinions, prejudices, and aversions—even if you try your damnedest to keep them to yourself. And as a human with life experiences, which is a tactful way of saying "baggage," you can bet your ass that from time to time your humanness will cloud your objectivity.

So how objective do you think you're capable of being? Can you keep yourself detached from your clients and their problems? If you're going to be a professional, you should have the ability to be completely and unwaveringly objective when you read for your clients. If objectivity is not your strong suit, it would be wise to devote yourself to mastering that skill with as much dedication as you would give to improving your psychic abilities.

Where do you think you rank on the objectivity scale, where *one* is that you can do a reading then go home, have a great dinner, sleep well and the next day only vaguely remember the reading and *ten* is you don't take payment for the reading, you call the client that night as well as the following day, and you take on their plight with as much gusto as if it was your own? To get a little clearer, here are a few questions to ponder:

- Do you tend to worry about your clients after the sessions?
- Do you fret about their situations and/or dwell on what they could or should do?
- Do you get yourself personally involved in some way?
- Has your own life—mentally, emotionally, financially, or even physically—been affected in any way by their troubles?
- Do you get angry or take offense if the client doesn't follow the advice you gave them?

If you answered yes—or even maybe—to any of the above, I suggest that you take a crash-course in becoming Teflon so that any and all client worries just slide right off!

One of the worst cases I ever encountered of a reader taking on her clients' challenges was when a tarot card reader came to me for a consultation. She was a lovely lady whose messages were all about how she needed to tend to her health, work to alleviate the aches and pains in her body, clear out the energies in her home (that's where she did the readings), and about the need to set personal boundaries for herself. The messages were awfully repetitive, and I felt like I was psychically stuttering. However, it all made sense when I asked her if she had any questions. From her purse, she pulled out a sheet of notebook paper with a long list of questions FOR AND ABOUT HER CLIENTS! Talk about taking on THEIR stuff!! And, no, I didn't take the questions.

Lacking objectivity can also leave you vulnerable to having one of your emotional triggers tripped. That happens when a client comes in with an issue that causes some angst—and be aware, it's not an *if* it happens, it's a *when* it happens. Unfortunately, not one of us is immune to losing our objective footing occasionally. Don't forget, clients come in with some heavy issues: child abuse, animal cruelty, incest, rape, etc. How much we're affected depends upon our awareness of the issues that stir up our emotions, and therefore, compromise our objectivity. Knowing what trips your trigger will allow you to either be prepared and avoid reacting or be able to regain your objective footing quickly.

This is yet another area where self-awareness is crucial to your business success. Without it, it's possible that your client's messages can get muddied by your "stuff." Not being consciously aware of it, you could become dogmatic about their situation or too adamant about how they should or shouldn't handle it. Whatever your client hears will be a product of your absence of objectivity. And that, let's just say, makes for a not-so-good reading for your client, a not-so-good experience for you, and it's definitely not-so-good for your business.

For issues that cause some discomfiture, there are a couple of simple tricks you can do to release the emotional charge of those issues. One of the easiest to do, is to momentarily stop, take a deep breath, and get yourself centered. An even better thing to do is to discreetly take your own pulse. That little act will get you grounded in no time—and it really comes in handy when you're being held hostage by someone who won't shut up!

In very rare cases, you might have to completely stop the reading. Excuse yourself and suggest to your client that they consult with another reader so they can get the guidance they need. In turn, recognize that there's a message for you in the situation, and that's that you need to get help with the issue. Again, this scenario is an extremely rare occurrence. Most often we're able to just get our human-self out of the way.

Here are a few suggestions on how to detach your human-self from a reading without actually removing yourself from it:

- Stop. Take a moment to collect yourself. Then ask your Spirit Guide(s), or whomever your source for Source is, for help in removing you, the ego-human, with the issue. Not to worry, you won't be relinquishing control over your being, no alien force will invade your body, and you won't be sent off to another planet until the end of the session! What you'll be doing by asking for assistance in detaching your human-self from the energy of the issue, is you'll get assistance to bypass your own emotions. I like to think of it as having a personal Sherpa leading me on a dark, precarious mountain road, where I strictly focus on what, and step where, their lantern illuminates. I don't look around and I don't look at what scares me. Whatever works for you to stay focused, do it to allow unfiltered information to come through for your client. In other words, you'll be out of the way so that Source can do its thing!

- If you're being challenged with a deep reaction to your client's situation, you can try clearing that energy by telling them that you're experiencing some angst. DO NOT, I repeat, DO NOT go into detail. You may, indeed, empathize greatly with your client, but by no means does that give you license to make them suffer through the telling of your story. No dumping on them—especially when it's on their time and on their dime! Most of the time, just verbalizing that you're having a reaction will discharge the energy and clear your "stuff" out of the way. Just as important, voicing the matter will alert your client that a lack of objectivity might've bled through, and with that, to take what you've said with a grain of salt.

- Worst case scenario is that your client's situation hits square between the eyes, paralyzing you in place. Again, this is very rare, but it can happen. We're human beings, after all, who, unfortunately, have unpleasant experiences. As a matter of fact, some experiences are so traumatic they leave a lifetime scar—especially an experience that was life-threatening. Psychics are not exempt from having traumatic experiences or being scarred by them. Even with lots of therapy and time we may believe that we've healed, but our woundedness has a way of revealing itself at particularly inconvenient times— like when a client is sitting across the table sharing a similar woundedness. If this is ever a position that you should find yourself in, honor what you're feeling. Be as kind and nurturing to yourself as you would be with a friend or family member, and, above all, recognize that you still need healing with that particular issue.

I am compelled to address the possibility of a worst-case scenario only because I've seen it in action. An intuitive counselor I once knew was fresh out of an abusive relationship and found it almost impossible to consult with women who were in domestic violence situations—and thanks to the Law of Attraction, she had a lot of those women come into her experience. When she had to excuse herself on more than one occasion, she finally got the hint, and got herself into therapy. Eventually, she got to the point where she was healed enough to take those kinds of readings and not get shaken up. She was then able to be in her objectivity.

If you should suffer a worst-case scenario and find it necessary to excuse yourself from a consultation, the good news is that you can expect that ninety-nine percent of your clients will understand. Moreover, they will appreciate your honesty and will respect you for it. On the other hand, you can also count on there being that one percent who won't understand—and just flat-out won't give a hoot about how you feel. These people are too self-absorbed to get it—or even care to get it. You won't want these people as clients anyway, so don't lose any sleep over them! Let me share a story about one of those:

> I once owned a metaphysical shop just outside of Albuquerque, New Mexico. On September 11, 2001, I was traumatized just like most other Americans, but New York is my hometown. I grew up there so the events of that day hit me particularly hard. I remember when the Twin Towers were built (yes, I'm *that* old!), I worked down the street from them for a short time, and I'd been in those buildings many times. Anyway, I opened my store and kept the television on all that day. Many of my regular customers came in, not to shop, but just for a hug, just to be in community. Then, a woman blasted into the store, completely uncaring about what was going on in the world. Any world other than her own, that is. She wanted me to do a reading for her because *"this guy I went out with was supposed to call me, but he hasn't called me, and I called him, but he hasn't called me back, and I just wanna know what's up with this guy?"* I told her that because of the events of the day I wasn't doing readings, to which she replied, *"Oh that, but that's not here, and I just have to know, like, what's up with him, because if he's not gonna call me...."*

My trigger got tripped. I told her to go somewhere else—no, not there, not out loud anyway! I did my best to remain in my objective space. The proof was that I refrained from telling her to go to Hell......or punching her lights out.

If you're living life, you can expect that there's always going to be an issue "of the moment," a thorn in your side, which will hamper your ability to maintain your objectivity. At any given time, we can expect to be dealing with one or more of the universal issues, which are relationships, health, career, and finances—and not necessarily in that order. These are, without question, the most common concerns for clients, but also for psychics themselves. We can't escape having to face each of these issues in some fashion or another at various times in our lives. Of course, it really sucks when they gang up and hit all at once—which they commonly do! Sometimes, even a psychic with great boundaries can be blindsided by an issue that a client brings to the table. Once again, thanks to the Law of Attraction, it's when we're in the throes of that very issue. Alas, even at those times, we don't get a pass to lose our objectivity. Not fair, damn it.

As a professional, maintaining objectivity is a must. From participating in psychic faires, I've witnessed psychics doling out advice that I knew was coming from their egos, their own biases, and from the challenges that they were experiencing in their own lives at that moment—definitely not from Spirit. What was imparted to the clients came from the psychic's own "stuff." I knew about their "stuff" because when we were idle together I was interrogating…..err, I mean, we chatted a bit!

The following are real examples of directives I've heard given to clients. (Sometimes it's not a waste of time to sit idle at psychic faires, you get to eavesdrop on the readings taking place on either side of you, which I'm now able to turn into examples for this book!)

The statements in bold type are verbatim what the psychic told the client. The names have not been changed to protect the innocent, because no names were used in order to protect my butt! What all of these scenarios have in common is that objectivity was nowhere to be found. See what you think.

Psychic Said: *"He's a jackass! You need to divorce him immediately!!"*

If he (or she) is an abuser, I believe we would all agree that the she (or he) that's being abused should, without any hesitation, escape from the no-good, lousy, nasty ass, son-of-a……oops, sorry, lost my objectivity for a moment! If he/she is, in fact, an abuser, Divine Guidance may tell your client that it's urgent for their personal safety, along with that of their children and/or pets, to get out of that environment a.s.a.p. If that's really the case, if that's truly what Divine Guidance says, then without mincing words you need to tell them just that. Abusive relationships are extreme situations requiring extreme messages. However, keep in mind that it's still THEIR decision to make. But, if the offender is merely a jackass, perpetual or occasional, there's probably no urgency to get away— and possibly no need to get away at all.

It's an out-and-out fact that there are always two sides to a story. Always, always, always. Be aware that you're only going to hear one side, which will be your client's side, so be careful not to get caught up in their victimhood. Unless, of course, both parties are clients of yours. If that's the case, the first thing I'd say is, *are you kidding me?* Beyond that I'd suggest that:

1. Make sure each one doesn't know about the other seeing you.
2. Be careful not to get caught in a tug-of-war.
3. Give much thought to who you want to get custody of you.
4. Disregard the first three and be proactive. Pick the party yourself that you wish to go with. Suggestion: go for the better tipper!

Above all, stay cognizant of what your role *is* in this situation and what your role *is not*. Your role is *not* of the friend they should go have a drink (or a lot of drinks) with. Your role is *not* of the friend they should sit around with (drinking or not) and bad-mouth the hell out of their used-to-be-significant other. Your role is *not* of a friend whatsoever. What your role *IS*, is that of the professional who they're consulting with for objective, practical guidance which is gleaned through your psychicness. No advice, and especially no directives, should be given to them from your human personality with all its own baggage. Your protocol is to be in your objectivity; stay in neutral and relay the messages to your client in an impartial manner.

When you can maintain your objectivity, you'll be receptive to a whole lot of information you might miss otherwise, whether it's advice for their legal dispute, a direction for relocation, if necessary, or, more importantly, for their healing process. If they're on the road to healing, you'll be able to confirm that, which will encourage them to keep up the healing work. However, if they're stuck in their "stuff," you'll be able to point that out—which just might be the kick in the butt that they need.

On the other hand, you might intuit that there's hope for a reconciliation. Your client may not be able to see any chance of saving the relationship at that moment. More than likely they're not receptive to even hearing that there's a possibility of saving it! If that's a situation you find yourself in, I'd suggest that you just keep delivering the messages and don't look up—it's a sure thing that you'll be glared at! But if that's what they need to know, you'll see those things if you stay in your objectivity, in spite of any glaring— or even some profanity!! That's especially true if they're stuck in relationship-rage, when all they can see is anger, blame, fault, a gun, a dull scalpel….

You can also be the instrument that Divine Guidance uses if your client needs to see—and take responsibility for—the role they played in the split. Despite the story they tell you, they absolutely played a role in the relationship's demise, even if it was from a past life. Only if you maintain your objectivity will you be able to deliver that message. Then they can begin the healing process.

Additionally, your objectivity will allow for messages which can help your client grasp where their relational behaviors—or misbehaviors—originate. Through you, they'll hear that their actions and reactions in their relationship come from issues with their mother (again, it's *always* the mother!), with their father, from the religion they were raised with, or even from their past lives—and you know they won't get the past life perspective from a mainstream therapist! Whatever the case may be, the unbiased perspective can show them—though maybe not convince them—that the "asshole" or the "bitch" you're hearing about is their best teacher. So, you see, without your objectivity, and if you get caught up in the ex-bashing, your client may be deprived of that wisdom and miss out on a significant lesson.

For instance, let's say a woman thinks her husband is being unfaithful to her, so she goes to see her psychic to confirm her suspicions, and to get some sordid details of the affair. She recites a litany of reasons as to why she's convinced her husband is cheating. But what if there's no affair and it's actually her jealousy and trust issues that are at the root of her marital problems? To glean that insight from Source, the psychic would have to remain detached and not get caught up in the client's story. However, if the psychic gets triggered and thinks about their own freaking cheating ex, she'd side with the client and tell her, **"he's a jackass"** and she **"should divorce him immediately!"** Whereupon, believing the advice was coming from Source, the client dumps her husband. That psychic did the client a great disservice.

Let's take this scenario further and say that after divorcing the husband someone new comes into her life. Guess what? Since she never got the personal insight she needed; she didn't heal her own issues, so she repeats her pattern with that someone new. And again with the next someone new, and again with the next someone new, and again with the next someone new.

In an alternate reality, where the psychic maintained objectivity, their psychicness would have told this woman that there was no affair. She would've been advised to take a good hard look at her insecurities, trust issues, and her track record. It's likely that she would've also been advised to seek counseling to overcome those issues. In this reality, the client was very well served.

As often as not, what looks like a nasty, unfixable break-up today might just very well be the crisis a couple needs to get help with. Most of us have heard the saying, *"if it ain't broke, don't fix it."* Well, people tend to look at relationships that way. What they forget is that for the relationship not to get *broke* in the first place, it requires maintenance, but maintenance is often the last thing on their list, after jobs, kids, watching television, looking at Facebook, Tweeting, etc. It's not until the relationship has gotten broke big-time before it gets some fixin'! Your objectivity can be part of that fixin'. And then they can live happily ever after—until the next time.

Have no doubt, there'll be many times when your psychicness will have to tell a client that it's in their best interest to terminate a relationship. At those times, carefully manage your delivery of the message. Say something along the lines of, "It looks like getting out of the relationship would be a wise decision," or, "At this point leaving looks like it's in your best interest." If there's a timeframe for your client to get all his or her ducks in a row, relate that timeframe. Let's be clear here, this isn't just about semantics, it's about the difference between giving advice and giving instruction.

Why should you avoid telling a client in no uncertain terms to break up? The short answer is because Divine Guidance wouldn't. Divine Guidance allows for free will and personal choice, and Divine Guidance stays neutral. Divine Guidance offers **guidance**, it doesn't give directives. The job of a professional psychic is to bring through divine guidance from Divine Guidance.

What's important to remember, too, is that people in relationships are doing a dance that needs to be completed by them in their own time.   If you relate guidance with any added emotion, your client may take what you've said as a directive, and end their relationship based on that directive. If they subsequently have misgivings, the blame for the split might then be shifted onto you. After all, you *told them to*. Furthermore, if the very-pissed-off *insignificant* other is told that the split was per your instruction, they may decide to hunt you down and send you back into non-physical! Be advised that Hell hath no fury like an ex that believes someone has meddled in their relationship!   Merely deliver the messages. THEIR decisions, and the timing of THEIR decisions, falls squarely on THEIR shoulders.   And then no one will want to kill the messenger!

Maintaining your objectivity certainly doesn't preclude offering help. By all means, recommend a few relevant books you think might help them, such as on love and relationships, health, stress management, or how to dispose of a body. Too, pass on the names of other professionals that might be of benefit to them, such as a marriage counselor, a therapist, a life coach, a divorce attorney, or even a shelter. Hand your client the referral's business card or brochure, then let them do what they want to with it. I keep stacks of business cards on hand just for those instances. I'd suggest you do the same.

Psychic Said: *"You definitely should not have that surgery!"*

When discussing a client's health decisions, the word "definitely" is only acceptable when it's used to mean that all decisions are *definitely* the client's to make, and *definitely* not yours to make for them. Definitely.

In a consultation about a health matter of any kind, whether it's physical, emotional, or mental, simply allow the guidance from Infinite Wisdom to come through, then let your client make their own decisions about their health. That's it and nothing else. No playing armchair doctor, pharmacist, or God!

It's a different matter when one is a medical intuitive. Health is their specialty, and that's specifically why people with health concerns seek them out. Yet, even though they use their psychicness, many medical intuitives will get schooled in biology, anatomy, physiology, disease, as well as in alternative healing modalities, in order to have a broader understanding of what they intuit. Because of their expertise, they have more leeway in working with clients regarding health matters. The rest of us, however, must tread carefully in this area.

Even if you've had some health care training, or perhaps your "other hat" is one of a bona fide medical professional, keep in mind that when a client comes to you for a reading, your role is that of the psychic and not of the health care worker. If you want to offer advice, let them know that you've "changed hats," and that you've traded your psychic chapeau for that of the health professional cap. By changing your virtual head covering you're also realistically covering your ass!

The majority of psychics, however, work without any kind of medical knowledge. But even sans technical understanding of physiology or electromagnetics, most will be able to identify a dis-ease in the client's energy field, will be able to detect weak spots in a client's physical body, and even perceive irregularities in their brainwaves. Alerting a client to any deficiencies, imbalances, or tears in their auric field, can give the client a head's up about the status of their health before the *dis-ease* turns into a full-blown disease. Nevertheless, there's a distinction between alerting someone to a lack of wellness you see or sense and telling them that they're unwell. Moreover, regardless of your track record with health issues, you'd be wise to avoid diagnosing, un-diagnosing, or re-diagnosing, a client's medical condition or treatment. It can get you in trouble. Western doctors carry malpractice insurance just for this reason. Last time I checked, psychics weren't eligible to.

Alerting your client to a weakness you feel around them, calling attention to some anomaly you're shown, pointing to a dis-ease in some part of their being, is absolutely what a professional psychic should do. Telling a client that they **definitely have** a dreaded disease or they **definitely don't have** a dreaded disease is not. Frankly, that's irresponsible. So, if you think you see a brain tumor, don't tell them that expressly; instead, simply tell them to get their head examined.

Prescribing treatments of any kind is also a very slippery slope. If your psychicness tells you there's an abnormality in the body, or if the client wants guidance about what to do regarding the malady their doctor diagnosed, it's not unreasonable to offer suggestions with respect to remedies or treatments applicable to their condition. After all, when we do this work for any length of time, we garner a wealth of knowledge about health matters. So, share what you know, but only if you're prompted by Spirit. And then, to cover your butt, add the disclaimer that you're not a health care professional and make it crystal clear to your client that you're not "prescribing" any particular course of remedial action. However, anything too unconventional—or outright freaky—should be kept to yourself. Let me illustrate with an honest-to-God-you-can't-make-this-stuff-up story:

> During a session in a metaphysical bookstore, a client told the reader (it wasn't me!) that she had a medical condition for which she was on medication. Upon hearing that, the reader commanded—yes, commanded—the woman to get off all her medications and instead begin drinking peroxide daily. Seriously. She "prescribed" drinking hydrogen peroxide. She went on to sing the praises of her own health ritual of drinking peroxide, and commanded that the client do the same.

> Objectivity? Nowhere to be found. And the lack of objectivity was the least of that reader's blunder. Most grievous was being reckless with someone else's well-being. She knew nothing about this client's condition or her full medical history, nor was the reader a health care professional. Still, she gave a directive that could have, most likely would have, had very dire consequences.

> When the session concluded with the peroxide pusher, the client complained to the owner of the store, who wasn't himself a psychic, but he did have a vision at that point: he saw a big red flag with the word "LAWSUIT" emblazoned on it! The reader was fired on the spot.

> While she was packing up her things, she ranted and raved, trying to justify what she had "prescribed." She just didn't get it. Maybe her lack of objectivity—or common sense, for that matter—was the result of drinking peroxide. Hmmm......

The moral of the story is, don't be dispensing health care treatments—especially crazy ones!

Again, energy healers and medical intuitives have more latitude in this regard, BUT, even they will routinely suggest that the client take the guidance they've gotten and consult with the other health care professionals they're working with, be it their acupuncturist, herbalist, or oncologist. What's more, almost all of the healers I know say that they NEVER, EVER give a directive about a treatment or remedy. They simply offer what they know.

Although it's not in our job description to offer up treatment protocols, it is a duty to provide the spiritual counseling that clients seek when they're experiencing a health challenge, particularly if they're facing the prospect of having surgery. It doesn't take psychic powers to know the three questions you'll be asked by a pre-op client. They are:

1. *Should I have the surgery?*
2. *If I don't have the surgery, what'll happen?*
3. *If I do have the surgery, what does the outcome look like?*

Psychic powers also won't be needed to know what I'll say next, but I'll say it anyway, because it's worth repeating: be in your objectivity before addressing these questions.

It's safe to say that at one time or another we've all had some experience with doctors, drugs, or hospitals, and from any of those experiences we would've formed opinions, perhaps very strong opinions, that potentially could permeate a client's reading—and our opinions have no place in a client's reading. We're just the messengers.

For a client whose surgery looks like it'll go well, that they'll be all the better for having it, and that—oh yay!—their recovery will be a walk in the park on a late spring day, it's easy to be the impartial messenger. We all want those kinds of sunshine and lollipops readings! But, alas, that's not always the way it is. Every so often, you'll have a client whose surgery will look less than successful. Perhaps you'll see complications, or worse. Needless to say, that's the kind of message that can be a wee bit uncomfortable to deliver, but you have an obligation to tell your client what your psychicness is telling you. But in no way, shape, or form, should you emphatically and explicitly tell someone, **"You definitely should not have that surgery!"** Even if said tactfully, don't tell them not to buy any green bananas either.

Under those circumstances, you may wonder, why not? All things considered, it seems not only reasonable, but obligatory, to warn them against having a surgery with "alleged" dire consequences. Well, yes, it's very reasonable, and yes, you're obligated to tell them what you intuit, but the issue here is not just with the message, it's with the uncompromising words and the forcefulness behind those words. Those words were an irrefutable directive. So, what's a spiritual counselor to do? Well, for one thing, make sure beyond any shadow of a doubt that you're two-hundred-percent positive that the message you're receiving is crystal clear. Then, articulate calmly to the client that from your psychicness, your Spirit Guides, or whatever, something to the effect of: *it looks like the surgery doesn't have a lot of positive energy around it*; or, *it doesn't look like the best course of action at the moment*; or, *considering possible alternatives might be a good idea right now.* Above all, I believe the following words should be used whenever a client has health decisions to make: Get a second opinion.

If the outcome looks less than positive, but it's not, "that's all folks," stretch your psychicness, while maintaining objectivity, to try to get more clarity and specifics about what that means. After all, "less than positive" can have many different meanings. For instance, it's possible that the surgery will be technically successful but the warning is about post-op problems, like infection or bleeding, or it could be that their recovery takes longer than anticipated. Or maybe "less than positive" is just a way for Infinite Intelligence to get their attention. Perhaps they need to be more proactive or take more personal responsibility with the surgery process, like asking more questions or doing a background check on their surgeon or the anesthesiologist—or even on the hospital to make sure that the Angel of Death doesn't work there. Then again, maybe it's that their body/mind is out of sync, which could very well result in a "less than positive" outcome. Having that insight, they could prepare themselves, physically, mentally, emotionally, and even spiritually. Perhaps even, it's the opportunity they need in which to learn that they can create the outcome they wish to have.

If you're astrologically-savvy, help your client pave the way for a good outcome by looking at planetary aspects of surgery day. Rule out any adverse aspects, check to see if the moon is void at surgery hour, or if it's in a position that isn't conducive to the kind of procedure the client is having. Above all else, make sure Mercury isn't retrograde. If you don't know what that is, Google it, but in a nutshell, approximately three times a year for about three weeks, Murphy's Law is in effect, where whatever can go wrong, will go wrong—and it affects each and every one of us in our daily lives. There are many things that shouldn't be done during a Mercury retrograde, like getting a car repaired, signing legal documents, starting a new endeavor—so **I** sure as hell wouldn't have surgery then! A totally Mercury retrograde snafu could be something like: *"Doctor, we're coming up short on our clamp count. Do you think you might've left one in Mr. Peterson?"* Personally, I think there'd be a whole lot less medical mistakes if doctors would routinely check where the planets are and how they're aspecting before scheduling procedures!

Nevertheless, even if the sun, the moon, and all the planets were in mis-alignment, it's still reckless to tell a client that they definitely shouldn't go through with their surgery—or anything for that matter, like their wedding, or vacation, or the bungee jump off the Grand Canyon.

But now, what if, just what if, you happen to get the infinitesimally rare client that you see dying during surgery? My suggestion is that you don't tell them that. Here's why: First and foremost, it would be wrong to plant those seeds in someone's mind before they go under the knife. The mind is a very powerful engine, and if you tell someone they're not coming out alive, and they take that as fact or fate, that engine could shut down. Even if they pulled the Death card from your tarot deck or you saw the Grim Reaper in your crystal ball, that person still has the power of free will to choose differently. Or else, consider that maybe they need to die. We know that God works in mysterious ways, but so do our souls, and it might be necessary for them to die momentarily for a soul exchange to happen. It's called a walk-in—out with the old soul, in with the new. Otherwise, they may need the death experience in order to come back and appreciate their current life—or to write a book about their encounter with The Light. Or just maybe.....

As you can see then, if you tell your client definitively not to have the surgery, they might miss out on a priceless personal growth experience. It might even be an experience they're dying to have.

The best you can do for your client if the message is that the outcome doesn't look good, is to urge them—don't command them—to get a second opinion.

Psychic Said: "*You need to go in tomorrow and quit that damn job!*

Personally, I'm not employable and haven't been for years. So when I hear the horror stories from my clients about how miserable they are in their jobs, how they feel powerless and trapped in the corporate world, and generally, how much crap they put up with, I just want to scream: *Tell those bastards to stick it and get the hell out of there! Take your power back, for Christ's sake*!! But, alas, that would be coming from my personal perspective (which is the main reason why I'm unemployable). It wouldn't be coming from my psychicness, and I definitely wouldn't be in my objectivity.

When it comes to matters of business, finances, and jobs, I'm convinced that the messages we get are from Spirit Guides who were earth signs when they were on the Earth plane! You earth signs, and those of you with significant earth in your charts, know exactly what I mean, don't cha?! And anyone who lives with an earth sign certainly knows what I mean, am I right?! For everyone who isn't the former or doesn't live with the latter, it means the advice is usually soooo cautious, soooo pragmatic, and oh soooo frustratingly conservative! In one word: BORING! I know of what I speak because I live with a Capricorn, and I have Mars in Capricorn—both of us drive me nuts!

You can think the messages are boring, but what you think doesn't matter in the least to the earth sign spirit guides, because those are the messages that they'll often give you to deliver to your clients. Therefore, stay in your objectivity and deliver those messages—even if you're chomping at the bit to give them your opinion about what to do. As an example, say you're in a session with a client who's droning on and on and on about how he loathes his job, how he loathes his asshole boss, how he loathes his co-workers, how he loathes the commute, and how he loathes talking about all the loathing. If you get caught up in that torrent of loathing, just like the psychic that I'm quoting here did, you'll probably wind up shrieking, *"you need to go in tomorrow and quit that damn job!"*

On the other hand, if you fortify your energy field against the loathing-fest, and put yourself in neutral regarding his job, his boss, his co-workers, his commute, you'll be able to just do the reading for the client without thinking back to when you worked for an asshole.

Let's continue to use this guy as an example—even if we loathe to—and say that you see a new job coming in for him. As a matter of fact, the job looks like it's "right around the corner." That news warrants a *HALLALUEAH!* — but it doesn't warrant telling him to immediately quit his current job. We need to consider what "right around the corner" means, mainly for that particular client, because he's the wildcard in your prediction. His energy, his vibration, his variables, will dictate whether "the corner" is a short city block or it's long country mile away.

If the client is a wide-open, clutter-free, clear channel to receive, the job offer could come to him before the reading was even over. On the contrary, if he has some mental or emotional blocks or negative beliefs littering his auric field—and you can bet all that loathing is vibrational litter—that new job has to fight the loathsome current to get to him. As a matter of fact, until he cleans up his act, all he's going to attract is more stuff to loathe. You can also bet that it'll include you if he takes your advice to immediately quit his current job!

Timing is another thing to consider, in that your timing may be totally wrong. Even when we devote a lot of effort and energy working on the timing of the events we forecast, let's face it, time doesn't always cooperate with us. And, ya know, as much as we don't like to admit it, being wrong from time to time about time isn't out of the realm of possibility.

Those conservative earth sign spirit guides will rarely, if ever, direct a client to do something as drastic as to walk away from their livelihood—and they have the inside track as to the person's financial situation and whether or not the person has blocks to receive. But mostly they don't give directives because they guide, and we shouldn't give directives either. Unless there's abuse or something criminal going on in the workplace—like their employer is straight out of the movie, *Horrible Bosses*, is a Mafioso, or is a tyrant that enjoys yelling "you're fired!"—walking out is overall not the best option for most people. When your client is being told that it would be a good idea if they quit their current job, nine times out of ten those conservative earth sign spirit guides are telling them to get busier than a one-armed paper-hanger in finding another job first. A message that tells someone to quit a job immediately would come from a psychic's ego and lack of objectivity. Hence, one's opinions need to be kept to one's self. Even if it means blood dripping down one's chin from biting one's tongue! And I hate when that happens, I've ruined so many beautiful blouses.

The three examples above—and it was hard to limit myself to three—show how the words out of the mouth of an un-objective psychic can be detrimental to clientele; likewise, an un-objective psychic can be detrimental to their own business.

There's an old saying in business that goes something like, *you gotta give the people what the people want.* If you wish to be a successful psychic, *the people* are your clientele, and what they want is clear, unfiltered, unbiased messages from Source. They'll come to you for what they can't get from themselves: objectivity (really, who can be totally objective for themselves?). They'll come to you for what they often can't find in their friends, for they're the people who'll completely agree with them, take their side, and will happily engage in a bitch-fest with them! Friends placate friends, and that's the way it should be. What are friends for anyway? But being placated doesn't help a situation. Don't *you* hate it when a friend, albeit well-meaning, tells you everything is going to be alright when it seems everything in your world is falling apart? The words are appreciated, and somewhere in the recesses of your mind you know that it's absolutely true, everything **will** be alright—at some point, at some time, in some way—yes, it will all be alright. But when we're faced with life challenges, we need more than a platitude. What's needed is guidance from Infinite Wisdom—which can only be gotten by a psychic who can maintain their objectivity.

An intuitive counselor must be ready, willing, and able to look a fellow human being straight in the eyes and tell them what they don't want to hear and what their friends cannot bear to tell them—if that's Spirit's message. If they're praying for a miracle regarding their own health or that of a loved one, but it doesn't look like a miracle is going to happen, you'll have to tell them so. It might be regarding a broken relationship that they desperately want to mend, but if it doesn't look like it's mendable, you'll have to tell them so. Perhaps it's a looming financial predicament, i.e., a bankruptcy, a home foreclosure, their business closing. They may tell you that they're doing everything possible to avoid one of those outcomes, but it appears the avoidance will not be. You'll have to be objective enough to tell them that.

Everyone wants their troubled circumstances to be resolved yesterday, if not sooner. But for some of your clients you might intuit that it's another several weeks, months, or even years, before they're out of the woods. Are you able to tell them that their intense situation will only intensify and that they should prepare for it to get worse? Can you be objective enough to deliver those messages even if they're sobbing uncontrollably across the table from you? Of course, being objective doesn't mean you shouldn't have compassion. By all means, offer a shoulder and some comfort—along with as many tissues as they might need.

Personally, I think an even more challenging scenario is when someone comes bouncing in, just as happy as a lark, and you see the bottom falling out from under them. That's when we have to put on the bubble-buster shoes, even if they're not a comfortable fit. (Oh, how I hate those shoes.) Nevertheless, a joyful, laughing, carefree client sitting in front of you shouldn't stop you from delivering any ominous messages. You mustn't feel guilty about pooping on their good mood either, because after all, the poop is coming from Spirit. But if you need to feel better about being the bearer of poopy news, look at it this way: the message you deliver now might squelch their happy mood for the moment, but by getting the warning, they can brace themselves for what's coming. Better yet, they'll then be able to take whatever measures possible to avoid the challenge entirely. As the saying goes, "to be forewarned is to be forearmed." It's your job to warn so they can arm, and thereby get back to being happy-go-lucky again—and lucky because they consulted with you.

Of course, not all messages are of doom and gloom. But those are the ones we tend to have a harder time delivering, and a tougher time staying in our objectivity with—unless you're a heartless, narcissistic, sociopath, that is, but you're not. We know this because if you were you wouldn't be reading this book. Instead, you'd be reading the biographies of Ted Bundy or Bernie Madoff or Donald Trump.

With your "regulars," meaning those clients you see often and with whom you've established a good working relationship, it's more than okay to ask them to give you a quick update about some of the things you discussed. You probably want to know if they got the job, how the surgery went, did they find their cat, was the date a love connection, etc., so encourage a **quick** email, text, or voicemail. In that way, you can be updated—you *are* part of Team Client, after all. But emphasize the operative word, which is "quick." That way, you maintain your detachment to their situations, and in turn, will then allow you to be in your objectivity in their future readings. It's not being objective—and certainly not healthy—to get actively involved with your clients' challenges or to step-by-step coach them through those challenges. If hands-on involvement or coaching is something you wish to do, I'd suggest that you get yourself certified as a life coach. Keep in mind, though, that even life coaches must maintain boundaries and objectivity.

From time to time, you'll form special connections with particular clients. You might even wind up becoming close friends. In those cases, be willing to lose a client. That's not always the case, but when you have an emotional attachment to someone it can pose a challenge to be an objective observer. If you're able to emotionally detach, you won't have trouble reading for them. But for many of us, that's not an easy thing to do. Personally, my objectivity has been known to falter—outright fail, actually—in doing health readings for people I cared about.

On account of being human and what goes along with that, namely, being hard-headed and having an ego, sometimes it takes a two-by-four from the Universe to get our attention. Unfortunately, I have to admit that it took more than just one two-by-four before I finally understood the importance of detachment. The first time was when a close friend came to see me late one Friday afternoon asking me to do a reading. She was worried that something was seriously wrong physically. She had a doctor's appointment scheduled for Monday morning, but wanted some insight before then. "Sure, no problem," I said, but right from the beginning of the reading I struggled. In retrospect, I realize it was a struggle between my Higher Self and my human-self. The human-self loved her friend, so much so that she couldn't be objective, and instead, she put on her rose-colored, dollar-store glasses. Through those lenses, I told my friend that she was fine and not to worry about the appointment. Come Monday morning, after running a few tests, she was admitted on the spot into the hospital because she had several blocked arteries. On Tuesday morning, they performed open-heart surgery. Fortunately, the surgery was successful and she recovered well. I didn't, I couldn't, see it. Surprisingly, and appreciatively, she remained my friend.

A couple of years later, a still-too-stubborn and cocky me (it's the Mars in Capricorn thing) wouldn't admit that I was incapable of doing a health reading for someone close. This time a good friend asked me to do a reading after her doctor found an abnormality on her mammogram. Once again, right from the start I struggled with the reading—still trying to make those cheap rose-colored glasses fit. And again, I told my friend there was nothing to worry about. She called me the following week with the news: Stage Four breast cancer. After many months of grueling treatment, she was, thankfully, cancer-free. She, too, surprisingly remained my friend.

After that one, I finally got it. From that point on my motto has been "when in doubt, refer them out!" When someone near and dear to me wants a health reading, I now know to be mindful about how I feel. If I feel even an inkling of struggle, I know I'm not in my objectivity, at which point, for their sake and the sake of a friendship, I suggest that they consult with someone else. That way they're guaranteed a completely impartial, accurate, objective reading, and I'll just do for them what I do very well, and that's love and support them.

Undoubtedly, you will also have times when you'll have to concede that you can't read for someone. Still, being a spiritual counselor, you can offer them some good, sound advice. Advise them to listen to their body's intelligence. If they tell you that something isn't feeling right, or that they have a "funny feeling" about their well-being, tell them to listen to that as closely as they would listen to you (if you could be objective) or any other psychic. Advise them to get themselves checked out immediately and, of course, if need be, to get a second opinion.

Check in often with your Self to make sure you're maintaining your objectivity, because losing it is like falling asleep at the wheel. You don't know you're losing it until you hit a guardrail. Or worse, until you've crossed the center line into oncoming traffic.

In wrapping up this chapter.........wait.........hold on a moment.........I feel a metaphor coming on.........picture this:

Your client is piloting their boat (their self), and a storm has rolled in making for really rough seas (their life). They desperately radio in to the Coast Guard (you) and ask the operator (you again) a series of questions: *What do you see on the radar? Which direction is the storm coming from? How high are the seas going to get? Should we change our current course? How can we get out of the storm faster? Where will we wind up if we make a change in course?*

The Coast Guard operator (that's you, but you probably know that by now) can provide the answers to those questions from viewing the radar screen and from the other high-tech equipment at his disposal. But overall, whether they're going to weather the storm, whether the boat will come out of it intact or break apart and sink, whether they have enough life vests for everyone on board to survive, whether there are sharks in the vicinity, can't be predicted conclusively. There are so many variables and mitigating factors, such as the condition of the boat before they started the journey, whether or not they have enough fuel, their boating expertise, whether or not they're strong swimmers, etc. So, when the boater asks the Coast Guard operator if they're going to make it, the most honest and objective response is: I hope so.

There's no question that the Coast Guard operator wants them to make it. No one wants to see someone adrift in a storm, wrecking, or worse, sinking and drowning. But the operator can't leave his post. He'll do what he can do, and that's dispatch rescue vessels. But it's not his job to go out and risk his own life to try to save them. Nor can he afford to get emotional or panic, for that will only prove detrimental to his job, which is to offer guidance to the boater.

The bottom line is that this dire predicament is not of his making and is not his responsibility. It's not his boat, he didn't decide to take it out that day, he isn't the one who failed to check the weather report, or checked and decided to ignore it and then went out in spite of it. The Coast Guard operator can only do what he is trained to do on his end to assist the boater. He'll send the call out to the rescue teams and provide the boater with all the information he has. Once the boater is given the data about the storm and the seas, and is informed to be on the lookout for rescue, they have to make their own decisions about what to do, like whether to ride out the storm below deck, to try to power their way out of the storm, or to get in a dinghy—or to jump ship and take their chances with sharks.

It's appropriate for the Coast Guard operator to offer up a silent prayer for them. Later on, in private, he can cry if he needs to. Hopefully, they'll be tears of joy, but they may just possibly be tears of sorrow. Either way, though, he'll need to then let it all go. After all, other boaters will be calling in for his assistance.

In the business of being psychic, one of your most important objectives is for you to be objective.

CHAPTER 4:

YOUR PERSONALITY

Who are we? Why are we here? No, I'm not mocking some Manitou Springs, Colorado, stoner-dude or an amnesia victim! Actually, those are a couple of deep, age-old questions that almost all thinking, soul-searching people pose to themselves at some point in their lives. Although they are powerful questions, I think the answers are incredibly simple. As for *who are you*? You are you. The original, one-of-a-kind, inimitable you. And *why are you here*? To be you, yourself, to create your own reality. I did say the answers were simple. The next questions to ask then would be: *Who is the one-of-a-kind you and what kind of reality do you create with that?* I believe that knowing your own personality—and being really honest about it—is a great big part of the answer.

There is a place for every personality and every personality has its place. For a happy and satisfying incarnation, we need to find the rightful place for our personality in a career path that's ideal for who we are and how we engage with the other inhabitants on this planet. It's got to be a right fit. The next question is whether or not your personality a right fit for being a professional psychic?

Generally speaking, with the right education and training, most humans can do just about anything they want to do. If someone wants to be a lawyer, they go to law school. If they want to be a nurse, they go to nursing school. If they want to be an artist, they go to art school—and get secretarial or construction training if they want to eat. But going to the appropriate school doesn't guarantee that they'll be a good lawyer, nurse, or artist. To excel, their personality must fit that profession like a tailored-made suit. Otherwise, it's like a poorly fitting, mismatched, outfit that's entirely the wrong color, which means that it doesn't feel very comfortable wearing, other people stare wondering if there's a mirror at home, and it looks like a fashion "don't" advertisement!

Consider the people we encounter where it's obvious that they hate their jobs—and probably their entire existence. We see it when we walk into an establishment and get "greeted" by someone wearing a blue vest who mutters robotically, *"Hi, welcome to this place."* Interpretation: *Why the hell are you here? If I didn't have to be, I sure wouldn't.* Or how about a cashier that doesn't look up at you but parrots the perfunctory question, *"Did you find everything okay?"* Have you ever answered "no?" I have. On very rare occasions I've gotten a concerned inquiry as to what I didn't find.

Sometimes it's just a shrug. Most times, though, there's absolutely no reaction at all. Then there are clerks working in government offices, for example, the motor vehicles department or the post office. Not all, but enough of them have earned the reputation of being less than stellar agents of customer service. I believe I've made my point.

To be a good spiritual counselor, a personality has to fit it to a T. Determining whether or not your personality is an exact fit for this work will require taking the time for self-exploration and self-evaluation. It's paramount that you're a happy fit for this work, but since you'll touch many, many lives in doing it, you've got be a fit for your clients as well. After all, if the psychic ain't happy, ain't nobody gonna be happy with the psychic!

Besides the great reveals, self-exploration is just fun! Don't we enjoy taking those goofy little quizzes that tell us what our likes and dislikes say about us, what kind of partner we're compatible with, what kind of animal or tree we'd be? One of my favorites tells you what kind of dog you'd be—and it's "Spot" on (good one on Playbuzz.com)! I'm not suggesting that any of these are even remotely scientific, yet some of them can prove to be surprisingly, even scarily, revealing, so says the Chow Chow.

For more *ah-ha!* and less *ha-ha!* there are any number of vocational and psychological aptitude tests available. Foremost is the Myers-Briggs Type Indicator Test. It's a psychology-biz standard that's been around for over ninety years. If you're not familiar with it, Myers-Briggs can provide insight into your psychological preferences, how you perceive the world, and how you make decisions dictated by those preferences and perceptions. I couldn't encourage you more to take this test. It won't tell you what kind of canine you'd be, but the findings will leave little room for doubt as to whether you have the personality to be—or not to be—a professional psychic. And to be or not to be is the question, isn't it?

Although these standardized tests list suggested professions, unfortunately, they don't include intuitive reader, spiritual counselor, medium, or psychic. Someday they will, but for now, we just have to read between the lines. If your results place you under the umbrella of health care workers, i.e., psychologists, therapists, life coaches, social workers, counselors, etc., you're a match. Ironically, when you're a professional psychic, you're not one of those other professions, you're actually a little of them all! And since like-attracts-like, you'll find that many of your clients will be psychologists, therapists, etc.

Unlike the olden days (before the internet), when the Myers-Briggs was only administered by counselors and therapists, now anyone can take the test online in the convenience of their own home, and without having to feel psychologically naked in front of another person! There are some sites that charge a fee to download the test, but there's free access to it on other sites. Seek and ye shall find.

To know who we really are, we have to take the time to have frequent intimate—and honest—conversations with our Self. We've got to ask probing and pertinent questions of ourselves. Questions like: *Who am I right now? Who am I meant to be right now? What is my purpose right now?* It's important to be in the now, in the present, so pose your questions in present tense. Which is to say, don't be concerned about your five-year, ten-year, or forever plan. If you follow the guidance from your Inner Being, your long-range plan is going to change anyway, so don't waste any energy over it now! We grow and change into our next **now**. We grow into who we are **now**, we grow into what we do **now**, and we grow into what our purpose is **now**. Therefore, ask in the now if your **now** personality is a good match for being a professional psychic—for now.

How easy is it for you to answer the question, *who am I right now?* Allow yourself to ponder that. Most of us will find that it's not so simple to answer. We humans have a bad habit of being many different things in many different situations to many different people. And it's all at the sake of hiding or losing our real selves. In your role as an intuitive counselor you'll work with many different people and many different personality types. Compounding that, you'll be exposed to, and working with, many different energetic frequencies. If you don't have a strong knowing of your Self, you can easily get lost. It's all about having a good grasp of who you are and holding your own—and you've got to be able to hold your own when engaging with these various and sundry energies. It's vital that your personality is one that is strong enough to handle all that.

I know, I know, I belabored the heck out of *finding yourself, man!* At this point you might be asking yourself, "Why is she droning *on and on and on* about finding yourself?" Well, if I may drone a little longer, I'll tell you. It's because your personality is a key component in being a good psychic and having a successful practice. If you're going to do this work well, you've got to have a powerful sense of who you are and who you're supposed to be with your clientele. If you don't, your energy can get sucked right out of you before you can even say Edgar Cayce. Is that a good enough reason for my droning? I'll continue then.

There are several personality traits that are beneficial to have in order to make it as a professional psychic. It doesn't need to be said that they'd be positive traits. I mean, after all, being disingenuous, rude, and obscene, won't get you very far in almost any profession......unless maybe a debt collector or U.S. President. But there are a couple of traits that, in my opinion, aren't just beneficial to have for this work, but are mandatory. The first one is honesty. Gentle, no-holding back, telling the truth, the whole truth, and nothing but the truth, honesty. That sounds like a *duh,* I know, but you'd be surprised how it's not always obvious when and where honesty becomes elusive.

When we can solidly count honesty as one of the anchors of our personality, it allows us to be able to say to a client, "I don't know," when we don't—and those are three very hard words for some readers to say. It also lets us admit our limitations and/or mistakes, because we all have limitations and we all make mistakes. Being honest means that the client hears the messages they need as those messages were meant to be heard, which is without any sugar-coating, tempering, embellishing, or personal perspective. And, chiefly, honesty can keep you in charge of the readings and unscathed by them. When we're honest with our clients, and with ourselves, we control how we wish to work, which means we only delve into what we wish to. That's important because, if you're like me, you don't want to tune into the circumstances surrounding the murder of a client's child.

The other must-have, foundational trait is strength, which means being in your power, emotionally, mentally, and psychically. Without strength, you won't be able to establish and then firmly maintain your personal boundaries with your clients. And without solid boundaries, you will, in no uncertain terms, experience burn out—fast. At various times and in various ways you'll have to draw on your strength. One way you'll need it is when a client is falling apart before your eyes. Depending on the circumstances, you may have to tell them to pull themselves together, or it just might mean that you hold the space for them to get it out of their system. It'll be necessary to draw on your strength when a client is in denial and continues to press you for a different answer to the same question, or when they're arguing with you for their limitations, or when they're pulling on you to get you involved in their drama. You especially have to stand strong when your client tries to "kill the messenger!" I mean that figuratively, of course, but if it's literal, fight or flight, baby! When you're in your power, you own and set the tone for all of your readings.

A trait that's not necessarily mandatory, but it's surely an asset to have, is being a people person. Having a genuine love of people does make sense since it's a vocation that involves working with people! Sounds like another "duh," but you'd be shocked at how many psychics don't get that part of it!! If you're doing this work, and especially if you're doing it professionally, you really should like people, care about people, try to understand people, as well as anyone can anyway! I'd just suggest that if you're not a people person, you might want to think twice before trying to make this your life's work. If you happen to be a medium, you've got people coming at you from both sides! But even if you're an animal communicator, you'll still have to deal with the critter's people.

That's not to say that you have to be an extrovert! On the contrary, introverts make great psychics—all that being quiet time, I'm sure! The thing about introverts isn't that they dislike people, it's that they generally don't like to talk much about themselves. And that's sure a plus when they're in session because they don't waste a client's time or a client's dime! The drawback for an introvert would be in promoting their service. Hell, self-promotion poses a challenge even for those of us who have a little bit of chutzpah! Frankly, though, a good psychic never has to worry about promotion. That's the Universe's job.

So, extrovert, introvert, or whatever the Meyers-Briggs told you, would you say that you kinda-sorta like people enough? Do you think people tend to like you? Are you good with people? Then again, have you given thought to how you'd know if you're not good with people? Well, it just so happens that I can help with that last one. Let's just say that you'd know definitively that you aren't a people person if you've ever received this sort of greeting card:

The caption on the front says: *Jesus loves you*;
when opened, it reads: *but everyone else thinks you're an asshole*

Being the recipient of that would be a HUMONGOUS clue that you're probably not a people person.

Fortunately, I've never received a card like that, but I once sent it (I'm not proud). In my defense, he was telling people around town that the woman who owned the metaphysical shop (me) was a Devil worshiper, and because he was a "good Christian," he was praying that I would get hit by a car while riding my bike to or from the store. In my opinion, he was NOT a people person, and again in my opinion, the card served to send him a subtle little message. I like to think that I was just the vehicle for delivering that message.

Hmmm, or maybe the Devil made me do it.

There is a definite distinction, however, between being a people person and in being a people pleaser. Becoming aware of that distinction could prove very helpful, especially if you're one of the latter. The former enjoys people; the latter is obsessed with gaining approval. Ultimately, the latter is consumed by that obsession.

Pleasers tend to do too many things for too many people, for too many of the wrong reasons, with too little time or energy left for themselves. A terminal Pleaser has a huge vibrational neon sign over his or her head which flashes the word "VICTIM" for all the world's victimizers to gravitate to. Consequently, the Pleaser is vulnerable to being exploited, or even worse, abused. The abuse can be emotional, psychological, financial, or physical—or, in the worst of the worst cases, all of them. It's no surprise, then, that Pleasers attract clientele that tend to drain them dry.

One way they do that is by their tendency to over-schedule themselves and accommodate more clients than they have the energy or hours in the day for. They also have a tendency not to use the word "no" very often. What's worse, is that they get themselves personally involved in their clients' problems. It's no wonder, then, that Pleasers manifest illnesses similar to their clientele. Shocker.

Let me make this very clear, I am in no way slamming, judging, or making fun of Pleasers, so if you are one, please don't be offended. The truth of the matter is that I think Pleasers are some of the sincerest, loving, and giving human beings on this planet. Unfortunately, they just don't allot much, if any, of that loving and giving energy to themselves. And therein lies the issue. So, I'm not saying that it's a personality flaw per se, I'm saying that it's a personality issue that needs healing if they're intention is to be a happy, healthy psychic (and person) that can continue to be a happy, healthy psychic person for a long time.

Of course, the most surefire way to resolve the issues will be by working with a good therapist, along with complementary resources, such as books, past life regression, breathwork, Bach Flower remedies, and so on and on. As it is with anything else in our lives that we wish to master, whether it's a new language, mastering our own lives, or building a prosperous spiritual counseling business, it behooves us to gather knowledge and get help from whatever and wherever we can find it. Yet, a lot of people argue that that can get expensive. Well, yes, it can—that's if you look at investing in yourself as an expense. Frankly, whether you're a Pleaser or not, making an investment in yourself is a wise one. But if you're a Pleaser, without making that investment you'll just continue to rack up expenses. Those would be the expenses to your physical-mental-emotional-financial well-being. If you'll look at it that way, you've got to admit that whatever the outlay of money is, it would be money well invested.

One last word of advice if you're a people pleaser: remember that you're a people too—please!

Now let's get back to more personality exploring and look at astrology. Most of us in the metaphysical world have dabbled a little with astrology, but if you've never had a bona fide, in-depth astrological chart done, you're missing out on a fantastic resource for self-discovery—and many "ah-ha!" moments! Should you decide to have a chart done (and you should, you should!), make sure that it's done by a highly-qualified, experienced astrologer. No disrespect intended here, but I'm suggesting a professional astrologer, not your friend who toys with it a little bit. Knowing when Mercury is retrograde—which we all should—doesn't make a person an astrologer.

Having a birth chart done **will** give you a comprehensive personality profile. You'll find your personal and professional strengths, and yes, as well as your weaknesses. A well-interpreted chart can also reveal other gifts and talents that you may not have known were dormant within, just waiting to be discovered and awakened. That kind of insight is priceless when we're looking to match our personalities to a vocation.

Of course, there will probably be a few revelations that you may not embrace, a.k.a., your shadow side, which are your darker character traits. Even if you don't embrace them you might as well look at them. Our shadows are nothing to be embarrassed about. After all, whether we admit to them or not, we've all got those darker sides to ourselves. I won't go into a long diatribe here about our shadows. I'll just say that the only reason a shadow remains a shadow is because we don't want to look at it. But when—or *if*—we do, we shed light on it, and then the shadow is no more.

An astrological chart will also provide much sought-after answers to the questions that people who you're close to frequently ask, like: *why the heck are you like that? why do you do those things you do? OMG, what's wrong with you??* Well, get a chart done and then you can just hand them a copy.

Another navel-gazer is a numerology chart, technically though, it's called a numeroscope. If you're not familiar with numerology, it's the science of numbers and their corresponding vibrations. In a nutshell, every number has a meaning and its own distinct vibration, and each of us has personal numbers. The vibrations of our personal numbers can reveal a lot about who we are, our potential, our challenges, what we've come into this life to do, and much, much more.

If you don't know a professional numerologist or don't know anyone who can recommend one, then head to your local metaphysical shop. They're the hub for metaphysicians. If there's a good numerologist to be found in your area, the staff will surely be able to steer you to them. If they don't know of anyone, then do what we do for just about everything else in our lives these days: go online. However, if none of the above pan out, you can still get a pretty decent, comprehensive numeroscope by yourself, and that's from yourself. There are plenty of most-very-excellent do-it-yourself numerology books available. And, don't freak out, even if you're not a numbers person like me, there's no reason to be intimidated by the thought of doing a chart yourself. Understanding numerology, thank the heavens, doesn't require the brain of a mathematician! And it's fun!!

So, if you're going to be a numerology DIY-er and you've got your most-very-excellent book, all you'll need beyond that is two simple things, which I'd put money on that you know. They are: your full birth name and your full birth date (the month, the day, and the year). Having a calculator handy would be a good idea—unless you DO have the brain of a mathematician! There'll be no how-to-ing given here, but I'll offer a very, very simplistic overview of how numerology can work for you.

Now, very simplistically, single digits are used, one through nine (although, there are Master Numbers, which are 11, 22, 33, 44, but I'm not going there because I'm being simplistic here). One of the simplest things to determine is your Life Path Number, also called the Destiny Number. The vibration of this number will tell you what you came into this lifetime looking to accomplish—besides the fact that you just wanted to come and play with all the others in your soul group! To get this, you add up the numbers of your full birth date and reduce them to a single digit. For example, let's use one of my canine daughters, Judy, who was born on September 24, 2008:

$$9 + 2 + 4 + 2 + 8 = 25$$
$$2 + 5 = 7$$

Judy's Life Path Number is 7. And that she so is.

Once you read the interpretation of your Life Path Number, I have no doubt that you'll see how crazy right-on it is about you! Then you can venture even farther down the numerical rabbit hole and do daily, monthly, yearly challenges and pinnacles, as well as the cycles in your life.

The letters of the alphabet have corresponding numbers, as well:

1	2	3	4	5	6	7	8	9
A	B	C	D	E	F	G	H	I
J	K	L	M	N	O	P	Q	R
S	T	U	V	W	X	Y	Z	

Using your full birth name, you'll get:

*Your Motivation Number.
This number is gotten by adding up only the vowels in your name and reducing the sum to a single digit. The Motivation Number represents what you consciously want out of life and what motivates you.
*Your Impression Number.
This number is gotten by adding up only the consonants in your name and reducing the sum to a single digit. The Impression Number describes your imaginative or dreamy side.
*Your Expression Number.
This number is gotten from adding up all the letters in your name and reducing the sum to a single digit. The Expression Number indicates your innate potential and abilities, and how you express them—or possibly abuse them.

Once you have your numbers in hand, all you have to do is read the interpretations of those numbers that are in your most-very-excellent book. And that's it. You might say doing numerology is as easy as 1, 2, 3!

In this chapter, I've given you some suggestions for your self-pilgrimage. What path you decide to take isn't as important as that you actually *do* your pilgrimage......pilgrim. So, however and by whatever means you choose to explore your personality, be assured that it would be well worth the time and effort you invest. Above everything else, the reason for the undertaking should be for your own happiness and fulfillment.

Of course, there's always the chance that you might discover that you really aren't suited to do this work, that the clothes aren't a good fit for you. If that's the case, yippee!! If that's what becomes clear to you, explore further and discover what **is** your right and true path!! And being on your right path means happiness, accomplishment, and success—and you'll look great in your new finely-tailored wardrobe!!!

Let's presume though that eHarmony and Match.com combined couldn't have done a better job in bringing your personality and this profession together and you discover that you fit the bill perfectly to be a contractor for Infinite Wisdom. Congratulations!!

And, by the way, only a personality like you can pull off wearing an outfit as fabulous as that!

In the business of being psychic, your personality will make or break your business; just as your business will make or break you. Make it your business to know if this is the business for your personality.

CHAPTER 5:

YOUR EGONESS

The ego is a subject that could be an entire book unto itself—and wouldn't the ego just love that?! Egos rule this plane of existence, most blatantly in our governments and in organized religion. It may be hard to believe, but egos run rampant in metaphysical communities as well.

Don't get me wrong, I don't think egoness is an entirely negative thing. I'm certainly not suggesting that it's something that we need to have surgically removed! The ego is a part and parcel of the human experience and it affects just about every aspect of our lives. Undeniably, our egos benefit us when we master it and when we make it serve us. The catch is to not allow the ego to become the master that we serve.

We need our egos for individuality and for our self-fullness. Our egos are who we're wearing. Say what? I equate the ego to outerwear. Let me explain. Think about watching award shows like the Oscars (ego-central!) where the celebrities are asked *"who are you wearing?"* and they proudly answer with the name of a renowned fashion designer. In this case, the celebrity is the spiritual being that is the real you, and when asked, *"who are you wearing?"* the answer would be that you're wearing the ego. In other words, in this here-and-now life, you're wearing the facade of *fill in your name here*, just as I happen to be wearing Viola in this life. So, you see, who we're wearing isn't a negative thing. What becomes a negative is when we forget who we really are under who we're wearing.

In all fairness, I believe that the overwhelming majority of all spiritual workers have good intentions and work in integrity. As a matter of fact, I'm privileged to be acquainted with many such individuals. They're wonderful people who bring their gifts to the world with an attitude of being in service, and without unnecessary hubris. Moreover, it's apparent by the ways they conduct themselves with their clientele—and with their colleagues—that they truly are connected to Source.

On the other hand, I've also known some spiritual practitioners who were anything but spiritual. These are the people that I'm discussing here. By far, they are the exceptions rather than the rule. But they're out there among us.

When I began studying metaphysics in earnest, I was as wide-eyed and as green as can be! For me it was a wondrous time of awakening. I was amazed by my own abilities, of the unlimited potential we humans have, of tapping into the higher dimensions of consciousness, I adored my newfound connection to Infinite Intelligence, and I was overjoyed about my Oneness to all people, to all living things, and rainbows, and lollipops, and unicorns......roll your eyes if you want, but I was a metaphysical virgin—and we've all been there! What's more, I wholeheartedly believed that if someone called themselves a spiritual worker, then, by gosh and golly, they were, in fact and in deed, a spiritual worker. I was convinced that the people who read all the right New Agey books and used all the spiritually-correct esoteric phrases, were highly evolved Light Beings who spiritually walked their spiritual talk. I just knew that if a person was wearing a crystal pendant it meant that they were a good citizen of the planet, that they lived healthy lifestyles, that they went around bestowing blessings on all the Creator's beings, and *la la la la la......*

While I did, in fact, experience a great awakening of consciousness, my naivety also caused me to experience a rude awakening to the workings of egoness! As a newbie to the whole being-a-psychic thing, I went to many local metaphysical faires where I'd stand off to the side and observe how the readers interacted with clients, which overall, was with warmth and respect. I didn't, however, think to pay any attention to how the readers were interacting with the other readers. Then, after about a year of watching and learning, while honing my own abilities, I summoned up the courage to participate in a faire. That's when I found out first-hand about the interactions between readers—and to say that it was a shock to my system would be an understatement.

Egoness reigned! I heard things like, *"Why is there another reader here, we don't need another reader, there's not enough business for another reader!" "His sign is too big, why is his big sign allowed?" "Why is her table so close to the door, that's not fair, people will see her first!" "How many readings did he get, why did he get so many readings?"* HISS-MEOW-EGO-EGO!!!!

Once again, I'm not saying that all psychics are that way, because the majority that I've ever worked with have been Lightworkers in every sense of the word. As a matter of fact, I'm not really talking about psychics at all, but rather about the egos that do readings. Big difference. I'm also not implying that people with big egos are bad people. Although, I do think that being a spiritual worker and having a big ego are strange bedfellows. Unless we're talking about a bed of nails.

How does your ego show up for you? Does it serve you or do you serve it? It can ideally serve you when you use the promptings of the ego as an impetus to achieve your dreams. It can serve you when you use the motivation of the ego to light a fire under your butt when you need it! It will serve you when it prods you to put your best foot—and face—forward. As a professional psychic, harnessing your ego and making it work for you will be a great advantage to building your practice and securing an exemplary reputation.

Who's running your show, your real Self or egoness? Pose these very pointed questions to your Self, but not to your ego—egoness lies!!

Do you believe that your way of doing readings is the "right" and "only" way?

If that's what you believe, then let me assure you, it's coming from your egoness. The truth is that there are countless ways to do readings. Frankly, if you believe that your own way of doing *anything,* whether it's cooking or painting a picture or praying, is the only and right way, well then, your egoness really has you bamboozled! For God's sake, that's the kind of thinking that perpetuates war on this planet. People believe that their religion is the only right one and that it has the absolute one and only true God. And that's just ridiculous. Everyone knows that God is an agnostic.

The point I'm making is that there's no one, right, true, hands-down, absolute way to do readings. For that matter, there's no right or only way to be a psychic or energy worker or spiritual healer......or human being. There's also no exclusive way of connecting to or channeling Source. The bottom line is that no one has a monopoly on Divine Intelligence. But let me put it another way, each and every one of us can have our own style, shape, or color of psychic Bluetooth, and just as long as we're synced up to Infinite Wisdom, we'll all receive the broadcast!

There are psychics who will argue that premise tooth and nail—actually, their **egos** argue it. They contend that their way, their Bluetooth, is the only way to connect to Spirit. Too, there are metaphysical teachers who believe that their teachings are gospel and must be precisely abided by—and God help any of their students who dare to veer from their instruction......actually, commandment would probably be a more apropos word. Don't get me wrong, though, many of these people are genuinely gifted and well-meaning. Unfortunately, they also happen to succumb to egoness of the worse kind, as in the following account.

Years ago, a well-known psychic (who shall remain nameless) came to my area for a speaking engagement. This was someone that I truly admired (up to that point anyway) and I could hardly contain my excitement! I mean, I was a full-fledged groupie! For me, it was like a Catholic meeting the Pope, or a Buddhist meeting the Dali Lama, or a teenage girl meeting Justin Bieber......or a teenage boy meeting Justin Bieber!! Needless to say, I was over the moon about seeing this individual live and in person, and I imagined that it would be an evening of enchantment and enlightenment.

Regrettably, the event turned out to be quite an anticipointment for me, and my admiration turned to disillusion—and distaste—for this still-nameless person. It started when I was given a handout as I entered the auditorium which had a statement declaring that this individual was a "real" psychic because they used nothing in the readings, such as tarot cards, etc. In and of itself that statement wasn't offensive. What was highly offensive, however, was that an entire paragraph was devoted to disparaging other "so-called" psychics. It was promotion, for sure, but it was, first and foremost, a very big ego. And, in my very humble opinion, that very big ego dominated the entire presentation. I say that because a good portion of the talk was spent building up their own psychic abilities by putting down, or outright mocking, other intuitive counselors. And I wasn't the only one with that very humble opinion, and the word ego was used quite a lot.

As I touched on in the chapter, Your Psychicness, when an intuitive uses a tool to intuit, it doesn't negate their intuitiveness (try saying that ten times). According to my online dictionary, the definition of the word "tool," as we mean it in this case, is: *Something regarded as necessary to the carrying out of one's occupation or profession.* That definition applies—and gives credibility—to any and all psychics who use some sort of <u>tool</u> when they work. The tool might be cards, a pendulum, sticks or stones, or whatever works for them, and thereby, their clients. Yet, sometimes it's an improvised tool, meaning anything that the psychic can get their hands on at that moment to aid them in getting their conscious minds out of the way, to get "into the zone"—or into the dimension or realm or space or vortex or whatever or wherever. Using a tool doesn't make a psychic any less of a psychic than one who doesn't use a tool at all. Furthermore, clients don't care if the psychic doing their reading is using a tool, just as long as the psychic goods can be delivered!

Besides the tools, all psychics have their own unique routines to approach and conduct their sessions, be it a little ritual they do, say a special prayer, chant, meditate, etc. If, prior to a consultation, you sit and pick lint out of your navel and then give your client a fantastic reading, let no one tell you your navel-picking is wrong! If that's your routine, if that's what gets your psychic juices flowing, that's what you should do. Although, maybe not let your clients catch how you prep for their sessions! Some routines seem reasonable, others may seem a little idiosyncratic—or outright weird. But who are we to judge? That's a rhetorical question. Only egoness sits in judgment because only egoness believes that only its way is the right way. With the exception of hurting or harming another being—as in a blood-shedding sacrificial offering—it doesn't matter diddly-squat what your routine is, what my routine is, or even what Madame-Gonna-Tell-Your-Fortune's routine is.

Similarly, many of us like to have items on our tables that hold some meaning for us, or that are sacred to us. On my desk, I keep a few special crystals, a rose-scented candle, a small St. Michael statue, and a happy frog figurine that my best friend gifted to me. You may prefer your desk to be naked, without objects or the energy of anything tangible. And you're right, your desk should be that way—but I, too, am right in how I wish my desk to be.

Cookie-cutter psychics would be b-o-r-i-n-g! Clients like variety, not only in the methods by which they get their readings, i.e., tea leaves, pendulums, bumps on their heads (that's an actual divining system), but they also like variety in their readers. Essentially, they want real people who are psychic, not Stepford psychics. An example of different is an oracle reader I know who's most entertaining—in a cute obsessive kinda way. Without exception, she starts out her consultations by emphatically insisting that her client plant both feet flat on the floor—and she'll check periodically throughout the session to make sure both of those feet are positioned appropriately, and she won't hesitate to adjust them if they're not flat enough! Then she has the client choose one deck for her to read from, out of about six or more that are laid out on her table. During the reading, and even though her client chose a particular deck, she'll pick out cards from the other decks as well. Different above all, and the first time it happens it's quite jolting, is when she raises her arms above her head and shouts, "White Light! White Light!" She'll do that frequently. I asked her about that once. She said something about needing to continuously infuse the room with white light. I nodded. But that's her thing, grabbing arbitrary cards and shouting, "White Light!" That doesn't make her any less of a "real psychic," because she delivers for her clients. And they keep going back and putting both feet flat on the floor.

Another psychic friend would insist on holding her client's hands for a moment before they began the session. That freaked me out in cold and flu season—all those germs, eek! But that was her thing. Sometimes she'd let go of their hands, other times she didn't. For the most part, though, after the initial hand-holding, she just spoke to the client. Oddly, she always kept a deck of tarot cards at her side, although she never used them and, obviously, didn't need them. Yet, they were always there. I was really curious about that. Since I knew her pretty well, we'd worked faires together, she'd been a reader in my shop, and had actually read for me without those cards, I asked her one day why she kept them there. Very matter-of-factly, she told me that they were there *just in case*. I knew how great a psychic she was and I can honestly say that if *ever* she had needed to pick up that deck of cards, it still wouldn't have made her anything less than a real psychic.

Those are just two examples of very "real" psychics doing their thing. Truth be told, having both feet on the floor, a moment of holding hands, or a shout-out to White Light, doesn't make them any less than real. As a matter of fact, I've seen those same psychics get asked an impromptu question and then effortlessly take a moment to tap into Source and give an answer. No one's feet got flattened and no hands were held. On a typical day of psychicing for them, however, they preferred to follow their routines and do it their way. That's what "real" psychics do.

Then there's me and my, shall we say, inimitable style. I make coffee, light candles, run the fountain, and play the same music that I've used for twenty-plus years. Then my client arrives (or calls) and I begin the reading. That entails slurping coffee—with the occasional spill down my shirt or on the desk—laying out Rune Cards, although I don't read cards and can't interpret runes, with my arms flailing about. I can be a bit animated and have been known to fling a bracelet off my wrist a time or two (but only once did I nail a client). Do I need coffee? Well, yes. *My name is Viola and I am a caffeine-aholic.* But no, not really, it's just my ritually thing that I do. Besides, I really love coffee. Do I need Rune Cards? Yes, because they are my "blankey," but no, because I'm the clairs: voyant, audient, sentient. Do I need to be so animated? Frankly, yeah, I have no control.

Now, with an M.O. like that, could I even begin to entertain the notion that my way is the only and right way to do a reading? Oh, lordy no! If it were we'd all be in trouble!! But that's what works for me. It's the way I'm most comfortable, and which allows me to do my best for my clientele. If I even remotely suggested that other readers should do it my way, it would unequivocally be coming from egoness.

At this point, I wish to add something about the still-unnamed well-known psychic. I believe that there's a reason for every experience and that, if we'll look for it, we'll find the lesson in those experiences. With that in mind, and after I got over my hissy fit, I reflected on the event and asked my Guidance what I was supposed to take away from it. The answer was that it was my own egoness I was to look at. I learned that if one has to disparage others in an effort to make themselves look better, then it's coming from egoness. After all, the ego views others as its competitors that must be vanquished! So, I had to admit that I was, in fact, enlightened that evening, and I got what I needed to learn—even though my ego would rather I *not* admit it. I see now that the Powers-That-Be knew that almost twenty-five years later I'd appreciate the experience and would be sharing my enlightenment with you. To this day, though, my snarky ego won't read any of that person's books.

Whatever you do or don't in your readings or use in your sessions, is right—right for you. And as long as you're imparting Spirit's messages to your clients, you're a perfectly real psychic. Just keep in mind—and out of egoness—that whatever another reader is doing or using, is equally as right—right for them. It is simply different. Respect the difference. Viva la difference!

Can you admit to being wrong?

Just flat-out, unequivocally, oops sorry, my bad, geez didn't see that, wrong? If you have a hard time admitting that you could possibly be even a little wrong, the ego is surely running your show. Let me break this gently to you: you will absolutely, positively, without any shadow of a doubt, be utterly and completely wrong from time to time. Your ego, therefore, might as well accept that fact and just get over it!

In Chapter 2 we talked about there being a myriad of reasons for a prediction you make not to come to pass, such as being thwarted by a clients' un-readiness for what they're asking or that they make very different decisions after the reading. Then again, and brace yourself for this, you might've gotten something wrong because you are, like any of us, a fallible Earthling! Whatever the reason might be, whether misinterpretation, lack of objectivity, or maybe you had a case of third-eye boogers, wrong is gonna happen. Regardless of why, know that it's just par for the course that you'll be occasionally wrong, plain and simple. Wrong, however, isn't something that egoness likes to admit!

Nevertheless, even if thou egoness protests loudly, admit it when you get something wrong. Of course, it's always a good idea to explore the why or how you were off the mark because then you'll be able to adjust the "receiver" accordingly and have fewer bad psychic-reception times. On the other hand, you may never know why. All you can do then is accept the fact that an occasional wrong is going to happen, push the bruised ego aside, and move on. Am I wrong?

Can you say the words "I don't know?"

For some, saying *"I don't know"* is almost, not quite, but almost as horrifying as admitting to being wrong. If you're someone who can't utter that simple phrase when you're stymied with a client, it's egoness that's preventing you. Contrary to popular belief, psychics aren't privileged to be omnipotent, all-knowing, all-seeing. Even the best of the best psychics don't know everything about everything everywhere and about everybody in every way every time! If we psychics knew "ALL" wouldn't more of us be big-time lottery winners? No, not really, but don't you hate it when people think they "gotcha" with that one?!

I think psychics themselves sometimes forget what their role is to their clients, which isn't to always have all the answers. Even if you're doing everything right, there will be times when the channel is choked off and the only message is that there'll be no messages. In other words, Universal Wisdom isn't giving up the goods. At those times, psychics and clients alike need to accept that every once in a while, even the best, most reliable and consistent psychic, will not be able to supply the answers that are being sought. Even more, there'll be times when a psychic won't be able to tap into the energy of a situation at all—and, by the way, if it hasn't happened to you yet, don't worry, it's just a matter of time! It just goes with the territory of reading for people—or not being able to read for people—because there's always going to be the incidental person who can't be read or one whose Inner Being isn't relating the messages to a third-party, which would be you, the psychic. That's when egoness has to be pushed aside, and the phrase "*I don't know*" is definitely in order.

Here's some perspective on a situation like that, which should ease any discomfort. Consider that by you not knowing, and thus, not being able to provide answers to a client, may just be the message they need to hear. You not knowing may be a crucial part of The Big Plan orchestrated by their Inner Being. We don't incarnate into these carbon units intending to have all our answers handed to us by someone else. Even if we say we do, we don't. We don't come into these lives wanting to be informed about everything life is serving up to us at every juncture. *Really*, we don't. Of course, we're not consciously aware that we don't want to know because we come into this existence forgetting all that, and all for the thrill of remembering who we are and that we have our own guidance systems. Therefore, in you not knowing, the client may be forced to glean their own messages from their own guidance system. So, in you not knowing, they're forced to go within. You could say, then, that by you not knowing, you're giving them a great gift. Don't leave them hanging, then, waiting for you to come up with their answer, just tell them that you *don't know* so they can get to work a.s.a.p. Eventually, maybe not in the short-term, the carbon unit will thank you—and your egoness can eat that up!

Trust Source. Saying *"I don't know"* to a client just might be a blessing in disguise. Perhaps, on a soul level, they chose you to be honest enough to say those words to them so that they could learn to tap into their own inner guidance. I think that sounds like a plausible reason, doesn't it? But honestly, **I don't know!** See there, I said it!!

Do you give thanks and appreciation where thanks and appreciation are due?

Some psychics are soooo impressed with themselves, and what they alone are able to do, and how their clientele is soooo lucky to have them as their psychics. That attitude packs a lot of egoness, and, unfortunately, it's not as unusual in the metaphysical world as you might think. In the spirit of full disclosure, I have to admit that I've worn that little crown of egoness before—and it's not pretty.

Don't get me wrong, we should absolutely take pride in our work, in our gifts, and in our selves. We deserve to take a bow for having the willingness and fortitude to do this work, when we could've just as easily have chosen a placid profession, like donning a blue vest and repeating robotically, *Hi, welcome to this place.* We're entitled to feeling satisfaction every time we're given the privilege of helping someone through our gifts. Notwithstanding, we have to give credit where credit is due—and that's to Source, which, as the name implies, is our power source. And you'd better believe that without our connection to it, we got nothin'.

I'll share a funny story about my friend, Carol, who, when she first got started, had a momentary lapse of connection and thought that she was a "solo act":

As Carol told it, she wasn't very busy for the first several faires she worked, so she'd spend the time observing the other readers to see what they did and how they did it. One popular reader that Carol was fascinated by read tarot and would snatch up a card, hold it to her forehead, and go trance-like. Carol said that it looked *"kinda cool,"* and she thought that maybe doing that herself might liven up her own readings a little bit, so she decided she'd give a little showmanship a try. When the next client sat down, she started the reading like she normally did, which was relying on her clairaudience, as well as tarot, then she thought it would be a good time to throw in a little drama. As she told it, she paused in a most theatrical fashion, she deliberately picked up a tarot card and very, very slowly raised it to her forehead. She said that she closed her eyes and waited. And waited and waited and waited. Nothin'......zippo.......zilch........nada..... Finally, she heard, *"Are you kidding? Do you think a piece of paper slapped to your head is how you receive us? When you stop trying to put on a show, we'll resume."* It was her spirit guides, The Boys, she called them. They'd have none of it! Sheepishly, she opened her eyes, put the card down, and the reading continued. She never pulled that ego-driven stunt again!

Actually, Carol was the posterchild for egoness-less. She exemplified a psychic just doing the job. Although her abilities were phenomenal, she never let it go to her head, and she never stopped being grateful to God (she was Catholic) for being able to do the work. She'd show up to psychic faires and stand out from all the other readers—but not because she was decked out in a flamboyant, glittery, woo-woo outfit. Oh no, on the contrary, her wardrobe was always most understated and ordinary. As a matter of fact, she looked more like a member of a bowling league or a convenience store clerk! Carol had a Leo Ascendant, which meant she liked doing things in a big way: big hugs, big greetings, big laugh, big heart. But never, ever did she operate from a big ego. She made her transition several years ago on New Year's Eve. I believe she chose that day because it's a big holiday. Okay, so maybe she had some egoness there!

When we sign up to do this work, it's a joint venture with Source. Remember, we might be the beautiful, high-flying eagles, but Source is the wind beneath our wings. Wow, aren't those some great words I just came up with?!

Finally, the most important question of all:

Why have you chosen to answer the calling/do this work?

Before answering that question, be sure that you know beyond a shadow of a doubt that you were called to do this work, or else it's a moot point. If there's no doubt shadow, then ask yourself if you've chosen this work to be in service to others or to have your ego stroked? That's a bit harsh, I know, and because I'm psychic, I also hear some profanity directed at me, along with a few Saturn fingers being raised (if you haven't guessed, it's the middle one)! But that's a valid question and one that should be to pondered and answered honestly. There's no question that by choosing this path should you make a good living, that you should get personal satisfaction, and it should bring you great joy. But most of all, it should be about being in service.

One last and very salient point I'd like to make regarding egoness and this work and that is that we NEVER, EVER, EVER earn bragging rights. Ever. In no uncertain terms is it acceptable to break the confidentiality of your clients' readings. In no uncertain terms is it ever acceptable to disclose that you've read for a prominent figure, i.e., a celebrity, a political figure, or someone well-known in your community. Not a word, never, ever, regardless of how important the ego feels.

Each and every session should be cloaked in a shroud of privacy and your lips sealed in secrecy. You and your client are enveloped in a cone of silence—or, as I like to call it, the condom of silence. Your clients will bare their souls to you and entrust you with their deepest, darkest secrets. There will be times when the sessions will take on the air of a confessional. (If you're not Catholic, a confessional is a dark, creepy wooden structure in which you're made to kneel, "confess" that you've cursed, said the Lord's name in vain, played with yourself, etc., essentially, you've been human. For that, you're told to do penance (3 to 500 Hail Mary's) by a guy sitting there doing who-knows-what, a.k.a., being human.)

Clients will confide in you very personal and intimate details of their lives. That means any and all areas may be laid bare to you: the emotional, mental, financial, spiritual, and even sexual. What they share with you should be considered sacred and privileged communication, and each and every little syllable of it goes with you to your grave or cremation oven.

Obviously, I have a very strong opinion about this. That's because I've been around readers who, in their effort to appear important, would disclose very private information about clients, divulge the identity of the clients, and even worse, would laugh at what the client shared in confidence. That's behavior that is not just unprofessional, it's indecent as a human being, and it's egoness at its ugliest.

Although, maybe there is one exception to breaking the condom of silence, and that's if someone comes to you, confesses to a murder they committed, and then tells you where the body is buried. Yeah, under those circumstances, I'd have to say that it's more than okay to break that confidence.......and call the police........but only after the murderer leaves, so that another psychic doesn't have to find your body. In a case like that, encourage the ego to do what it does best and save its own ass!

In the business of being psychic, ditch the egoness. Your clients don't need to hear you brag about how great you are. Your job is to remind them of how great THEY are and how much greater they are capable of being. They will express their gratitude to you by referring you to others and by returning to you again and again.

CHAPTER 6:

YOUR WEIRDNESS

Let's face it, "normal" people think we're weird. Supposedly, as per "normal" people, our weirdness can be attributed to brain mis-firings, being descended from a long line of gypsies, a connection to extra-terrestrials, or even that we have an, as yet undiscovered, weird chromosome in our strains of DNA—and that's from the people who like us! The "normals" that would like to have burning at the stake reinstated believe that the likes of us are possessed by demonic forces. Such being the case then, to be intentionally weird simply for weird's sake is unnecessarily weird!

What does weird mean anyway? Personally, I think being weird is a good thing when it's a positive expression. The flip side of that, the negative, is being pretentiously bizarre or outrageous. Out of my dictionary, the definition of the word "weird" is: *"of, relating to, or suggestive of preternatural or supernatural; of a strikingly odd or unusual character; strange."* It sounds like a label that's placed on things that are not understood by "normal" people. For those that are ready to build a pyre to burn our asses, weird is feared.

Jokingly, I call clients who've never had a reading "virgins"—and I love it when they come to see me, purely for the entertainment factor! I love to watch the expression on the person's face as they walk into my office. Since they're usually not sure what to expect, they're plainly surprised by what they see—or, rather, what they don't see. They don't find me wearing a turban, I'm not in a pitch-dark room breaking fire codes with a preponderance of burning candles, I'm not chanting and whispering conspiratorially about spirits and curses—and I'm only exaggerating a little bit! Seriously, more times than I can count, subsequent to the reading, a client has literally said to me that they didn't expect me to be so "normal!" Funnier still, is that I've been told A LOT that they expected that I'd be more "spooky!" Don't be surprised how that stereotype will precede a lot of your meetings.

In spite of an explosion of television shows over the last several years covering anything, everything, and everybody dead (or undead), the weird stereotype persists. There's ghost-hunting and busting, spirit communication, demon-clearing, haunted places to visit, exorcisms performed live, crime scene energy reenactments, and so on. Some of these programs perpetuate weirdness and throw in an extra dash of terror and gruesomeness to increase their ratings and viewership. But there are a number of shows that are incredibly good at representing psychics, and the spirit world in general, in a positive—and less weird—light. They attempt to offer an understanding of the metaphysical and how working with the *para*-normal is not at all *ab*-normal; that instead, it's just another kind of normal. Essentially, they depict psychics as everyday people. Albeit, everyday people doing something weird.

A few years ago, there were a couple of shows, *Medium* and *Ghost Whisperer*, that portrayed the psychic characters as normal women, living normal everyday lives, and having normal relationships. Except for the seeing and talking to dead people thing, it was all pretty much life as normal. The character in *Medium*, Allison, was particularly normal. She wore baggy pajamas, sweats, and everyday clothes that fit, just like normal women. However, in *Ghost Whisperer*, Melinda often ran around in nighties with her boobs hanging out. Actually, her boobs hung out of everything she ever wore. That wasn't such a normal depiction for an everyday woman—and definitely not necessary for a psychic! I gotta say, she had great boobs, but that has nothing to do with psychic abilities!!

Then there's the *Long Island Medium* and her family. She's a hoot! She's someone who could be anyone's relative, a neighbor, even a girlfriend to go to happy hour with. In spite of cameras following her around, she's pretty normal. And she's really normal for a Long Islander.

Regardless of those shows, the weird stereotype still prevails. So, why, oh, why then, would any one of us want to intentionally perpetuate weirdness? We work with the paranormal, therefore we know how normal it actually is. So, shouldn't we behave accordingly and not be weird about it?! Yet, that's not always the case. Some psychics feel the need to hide behind bizarre props and exaggerated pretense.

To say that props and pretense only serve to bolster the weird label is an understatement. The worst part is that they project inauthenticity. The truth of the matter is that psychics have regular lives and do regular things. Things such as having to go to the grocery store or do the laundry. We have shit to take care of, meaning we change diapers for little two-leggeds, and clean litter boxes and/or scoop poop for the four-leggeds. We clean our homes—unless we're lucky enough to be able to hire a cleaning person—and, just like any other normal person, we—okay, I—get jealous of people who have a cleaning person. We have families to attend to, or deal with, depending on the relationships. When we get sick, and we all do from time to time, we vomit and have diarrhea like every other regular being on the planet. That's probably a bit too graphic, but hey, that's real life. That's a normal authentic life. Considering all this normal-ness, acting as if we descend into our sessions from another realm and then ascend back to it afterward is anything but authentic. That's just weirdness.

What I'm saying is that, for the most part, we psychics lead pretty average lives. The only exception is that our life paths, our career paths, what we do for a living, isn't considered a normal mainstream profession, yet it'll never be considered one if we perpetuate the oddball status.

Psychics who have "made it" get that. What I mean by that is a psychic that has gained recognition and credibility (as opposed to notoriety) through the media, such as having their own television show or being featured on one, who has had their book(s) successfully published, or those who have been written about for their successes like their participation in scientific experiments or for being instrumental in solving police cases. When I say that they get it, I mean that they're confident in their abilities and secure in their connection to Infinite Intelligence. Most of all, they know that their abilities aren't a result of what they're shrouded in or how many crystals they adorn themselves with. They look and act like everyday people. They're authentic.

Therefore, be yourself. If you're anything other than that, your clients will know. You may be the psychic, but don't underestimate for a minute how intuitive your clients are. Consciously or subconsciously, your clients will recognize if you're not being authentic—and sensing that may very well diminish their trust in you. The best and only way to be, is to be yourself.

Also bear in mind that it's not just your own authenticity that's at stake here. To each and every person that comes to see you, you represent what being a professional psychic is and what a professional psychic looks like. No pressure though.

Let's not forget either that we are teachers. We don't just sign on to do this work to make predictions. Of course, that's a big part of it, but it's not the whole job description. We're also here to teach people how to find and develop their own inner awareness. We're here to teach people that it's beneficial—and normal—to tap into and listen to their own guidance, their own psychicness. We won't accomplish that by acting, looking, or being weird!

Being unnecessarily weird is far different than having a few personality quirks or idiosyncrasies. As I said in the previous chapter, it's normal for all psychics to have their own little "ritually" things that they do before, during, or after sessions. Those things aren't weird if they're genuinely a part of the psychic's process. On the contrary, sometimes it's a performance instead of a process, and that's when it's pretentious— and it's amping up the weird. For example, having a huge altar with statues of umpteen saints and scores of lighted candles is one thing, because if saints-on-fire is your thing, so be it. But to stand before the altar after the client is seated and mumble and genuflect for several minutes, is something else entirely. It's phony—and a little unnerving. That, my friends, was *my* first experience with a psychic.

What image do you project to the clients who consult with you? Who do you wear? Is it really and truly your everyday mode of fashion to wear a High Priest/Priestess crown, to be bejeweled from head to toe with crystals and amulets, to sport copper headgear, or to dress in flowing robes? If it's really and truly your style, by all means, go for it. If that's the authentic you, it won't seem weird because your authentic self will shine through. But I ask you, and you should ask yourself: Do you ordinarily go to the grocery store in that attire? Would you go out on a date wearing that? Would you hang out with your non "woo-woo" friends in those duds? Would you wear that outfit to your Grandma's for Thanksgiving? If not, why not? There you go.

If you've worked, or still do work, in the corporate world, you know that there's an emphasis on appearance and dressing for success. Any company that employs you will consider you to be a representative of their company; therefore, you're expected to wear the appropriate attire in order to present the image that the company wants to project. If you want to keep your job, you must comply with the mandatory dress code. Consequently, you comply and dress accordingly. Besides merely wanting to keep your job, it's reasonable to say that you adhere to that standard of dress to be taken seriously and to be viewed as a professional. With that in mind, take yourself seriously in your capacity as a psychic and present yourself as a professional.

Granted, it seems like we're comparing apples and oranges because doing psychic readings is a far cry from the corporate world—thank God & Company! And granted, you are, in fact, self-employed and can freely and happily do your own thing. But just because you're doing your own thing doesn't mean it's such a good idea to swing completely to the other end of the fashion spectrum to "way-out-there" weird—and not weird in the positive sense! What is way-out-there weird, you ask? It's looking something like a New Age Liberace, it's Elton John in the 70's, it's an advertisement for Roswell, or it's a fortune-telling Lady Gaga! Better yet, think Walmartians!! Ya know, come to think of it, I bet it's at Walmart that Lady Gaga gets her costume ideas!!!

What I'm suggesting is to present yourself in a manner that your clients can relate to. Or, at the very least, a manner that doesn't frighten them! Be relaxed, be comfortable, but also be, dare I say it, relatively normal. As much as we may not like to admit it, we judge people, and we are judged by other people, by how we look—and how we look is the impression we make.

Speaking of impressions, before you're even face-to-face with a potential client, the first impression you make is with your name. We're identified by our names, we're recognized by our names, and an impression about us WILL be made by our names. That impression may not be such a favorable one if what we call ourselves is weird and/or inauthentic.

There isn't much we can do about a strange or unusual name that was given to us at birth. Or an antiquated one, say like, *Viola*! In my case, I didn't embrace the name until I was an adult, and now just use it singularly. It's not because I'm trying to be weird either. My reasoning is, first off, there aren't that many Violas around who are psychics, so anyone who Googles my name can find me pretty quick. But mostly, it's because with a name like Viola, who needs to use a last name? I mean, it's kinda like Cher, or Oprah, or any one of the seven dwarfs.

Whether strange, unusual, or antiquated, most people just get used to their names or grow into them. If a person doesn't feel a true resonance with their name or doesn't think their name has a good numerological vibration to it, they could tweak it or change it up, perhaps use initials or a spelling variation. Of course, if someone really doesn't like their name, there's always the option to change it to something different. And that's no big whoop, right? Well, actually, it's not always whoopless with the metaphysically-inclined. Some of these folks espouse names that are pretty disingenuous or just flat-out weird.

Let me illustrate—and the name has been changed (ever so slightly) to protect my butt:

I had a friend who by day was an accountant and did tarot card readings on the side. She was a lovely Caucasian woman who became very interested in Native American culture, so she began studying their traditions with a group of five or six other very Caucasian women. The group chose an Indian Nation and embraced its ideology and customs. And these women *really* embraced it, not just in theory, but in what could also be considered role-playing. My friend even switched over to a Native American tarot deck. It was all very sweet, but then things got a bit bizarro.

One thing the group did was to hold a ceremony renaming themselves. Each woman came up with an Indian name for herself and each woman was very insistent that she be called solely by that name. And not just within their group, but by everyone: all their family and friends, as well as at their places of employment. My friend's new name was something like, Big Brown Bison Standing on Granite Rock Mountain. Really.

I'm a firm believer in "to each her own," but besides the name being way too long to say, Big Brown Bison Standing on Granite Rock Mountain (try it), it lacked one iota of authenticity. Too, I had trouble keeping a straight face when I tried calling her that—and, believe me, I tried!! Another thing that made it seem somewhat cartoonish was that she was a very tall, blond, blue-eyed, big-boned Polish woman complete with "vich" at the end of her real last name. Thus, Big Brown Bison, etc., wasn't just disingenuous, it was weird.

Call yourself and your business whatever you wish, but bear in mind that keeping it real will attract real clientele.

Fundamentally, weirdness will impede the growth of your practice because clients want to relate to you. They're not going to care what you do in your personal life or who or what you worship, within reason, that is. If your deities require the sacrificing of small animals or the blood of virgins, face it, that's way weird and people **are** going to care. Moreover, they'll probably call the authorities on what they judge to be your warped ass! But your clients will need to be able to relate to you. When we sit with our clients we're not just doing readings for them, we're also forging relationships with them. So, anything too over-the-top is anything but relatable.

As an example, let's take the topic of UFOs. According to polls, an extraordinarily high percentage of people believe in the existence of UFOs and extraterrestrials. Still, most people don't talk much about aliens—except in Roswell, New Mexico, where it's an all-that's-talked-about industry. For everybody else, unless they're in like company, they're hesitant to admit that they believe—and with good reason. Talk of aliens puts one at risk of being ridiculed or having one's sanity questioned. One will be dubbed weird. The subject of UFOs is a lightening-rod issue that can be quite, dare I say, *alienating*! – LOL, sorry, I couldn't resist that one! Consequently, even though it's a widely accepted, albeit unspoken belief, it's not overtly relatable.

Continuing with the theme of UFOs, here's an example of what wouldn't be considered relatable. Let's say that there's a tremendously gifted psychic, Eddie Thomas, E.T., for short (we'll make him a male because most space cadets are), who happens to also be a UFO-enthusiast. Furthermore, let's say that E.T. has such enthusiasm for UFOs and aliens that he has every inch of his consultation room covered with pictures of spaceships, has statues of aliens everywhere, there are inflatable flying saucers hanging from the ceiling, and he has an eight-foot tall green stuffed alien standing in the corner. To top it all off, his garment of choice is a Star Trek uniform, alien-head jewelry (I'm not making fun because I have some alien-head earrings—and I *love them*!), and other assorted UFO-related adornments.

Now, imagine that a brand-new client comes in for a session. Unless that client is another UFO aficionado, when they enter the

UFO-atorium, that client will only be seeing and thinking one thing: *weird*. Wait, maybe two things. The other would be: *beam me the hell out of here, Scotty*. Unfortunately, in this scenario, because the client couldn't relate to E.T., the insights he could've offered the client would be lost in space.

That's not a completely fabricated scenario. I've blown it a bit out of proportion, and only in that I've never encountered anyone in a Star Trek uniform. But I have had several experiences with readers where I thought I might've stepped into another time, a different dimension, or a fantasy land. Whatever or wherever it was, I couldn't relate to it. The bottom line is, to grow your business, everything should be in moderation so that the average client can relate to you.

Building a successful, relatable, practice also requires that we weird-proof what we say and how we say it. It's important to gauge the client sitting across from you. In other words, you've got to know your audience. So, again using an alien analogy, it wouldn't be appropriate for E.T. to start talking to a client he wasn't familiar with about how some public figures are aliens, that some of their friends and acquaintances are from other planets or dimensions, and that he's excitedly awaiting the mothership to come and pick him up.

Unless you know your client well and you're absolutely certain that they're receptive to what you believe in, speaking outside their understanding or belief system will only cause a disconnect between the two of you. You also may horrify them. He or she may be expectantly looking up at the sky, but it's not for a mothership. They may, instead, be waiting for the Rapture and on the lookout for Jesus to surf down on the clouds to retrieve The Chosen. Of course, at that point, they judge you as not one of them. I admit, that's a wacky exaggeration. I mean, really, Rapture believers aren't generally known for seeking out the counsel of psychics.

If you're not one-hundred and fifty percent certain about what the person in front of you believes, worships, or ascribes to, it would behoove you to keep your theology, theosophy, or your theory of the universe to yourself. Otherwise you will accomplish two things that you probably didn't intend to:

1. You will lose a client;

2. You perpetuated the "psychics are weird" stereotype. Hey, thanks a lot.

I would venture to say that ninety-eight percent of the people that come for a consultation are wanting advice from Infinite Intelligence about very secular matters regarding the very secular lives that they're currently living. Knowing that, play it safe and stick to using secular language and philosophies. Until you know where they are in their spiritual leanings, it would be best to refrain from launching into how they're living parallel lives on other planets and in other dimensions. If they don't believe in those things, it will be too weird for them and you will most likely run them off. Only if you get an emphatic "YES!" when you ask if they believe in past lives, should you begin telling them that they're working off karma from a past life in Transylvania where they were a henchman for Vlad the Impaler. If you get a "NO," skip it and move on to the secular stuff. Even though you tune into that lifetime where your client and Vlad were really tight, and your client was Vlad's highest producer, single-handedly impaling over a hundred human beings, if they don't believe in past lives, that tidbit of information—and you—may be too weird for them. Let alone gory.

Once again, it doesn't matter what you personally believe in. That's between you and your God(s), your Inner Being, your soul, your invisible friends. The suggestion here is that by, as they say, keeping your cards close to your vest, you'll not only develop a practice, but you'll expand that practice to more than just a select few. People have a natural desire to want to relate to someone they're working with, especially someone they're working with in intimate ways, such as their doctor, their therapist, their acupuncturist, their veterinarian—and their spiritual consultant. You will satisfy that relatability by being a bit mainstream in engaging with them. Even if it's a stretch!

Another reason to keep your beliefs to yourself is that some of your clients won't believe in much of anything—except what they can see, hear, and touch. You wouldn't think it, but there are a lot of people who consult with psychics that don't believe in reincarnation, aliens, a Higher Self—or even God, for that matter. But it's not our job to persuade them. If you try to ram your own beliefs down their throat, they'll just leave in a huff, and probably never return to you.

The majority of people that come to you will want to discuss belief-neutral topics that affect their present, physical, here and now, existences. They'll be looking for insight into their finances, their relationships, their health, and their career matters. So, listen to yourself speak to them. Talk to your clients in words they understand and offer concepts they can relate to. That will give you credibility and relate-ability with them. If you talk to them about things that are foreign to their world view—or a too out-of-this-world view—they won't really hear you, they'll just chalk you up to being weird, and thus, you won't be serving them. You won't be doing your reputation any favors either. Clients want *compelling*, not *repelling*. The following illustrates that.

A hundred moons ago, I became acquainted with an astoundingly gifted psychic. Her readings were jaw-droppingly, bone-chillingly, un-freaking-believably accurate, and she should have had a thriving practice. But one thing prevented that, which was, and with no disrespect meant, she was a loon. She lived in a dilapidated old house that reeked to high heaven of uncleaned cat boxes, and from carpeting that was used as cat boxes by many cats, many in-bred and continually-breeding cats. Many, many, many cats. After leaving that house, you'd drive away with your car windows rolled down, even in the dead of winter, get home and immediately take a shower, wash your hair, and launder your clothes, because you smelled like cat piss.

Cats were everywhere. Cats would jump up onto her table during readings. Whenever that happened, she would slap the table hard and holler "*CONFIRMATION KITTY!*" which was, needless to say, very unnerving. Cats would also jump up on the back of the chair that a client was sitting in. Quite a number of times the cat would miss the chair entirely. Instead, claws would dig into the client's head and back. She found that hilarious and would laugh maniacally. If that wasn't bad enough (and oh, it was bad), she would often go on rants about anything from how the Holocaust never happened to how, in great detail, she was going to regrow her teeth that had fallen out. She was truly weirdness embodied. How she never got sued or how the health department was never called on her is beyond me. But she did have a connection to Source, maybe that was why.

Whenever someone had a session with her it was impossible for them not to be positively awestruck by her remarkable psychic abilities. However, it was never the extraordinary messages they got from her that they'd later recount. It was always whatever bizarre and crazy things she had talked about. Or wore. For that visual, use your imagination—you won't be far off, I promise. Unfortunately, her weirdness always took precedent. What was really weird, though, was that I went back to her after my initial reading. Understandably, I was in a minority because most people didn't—particularly the people that had scars from the "confirmation kitties."

Risking my own credibility here, I admit that I not only went back to get readings from her, but I actually studied with her. *And I have the nerve to call her a loon??* But, I've got to say that she was one of the greatest teachers I have ever had. Under her tutelage, I not only developed my own abilities, but over and above that, I learned so much about how NOT to interact with my own clients, what NOT to do in sessions with people, and what NOT being a professional meant. I also learned NOT to let my clients be mauled by any of my pets!

Maybe you believe the Holocaust never happened, or maybe you plan on growing some new teeth. It's your right to believe that, and it's your own reality to create. You're entitled to have your convictions and to believe in whatever you wish to. Personally, I truly believe that if someone has unwavering faith, if they believe in their heart of hearts and with every fiber of their being, with absolutely no doubt, that they can, in fact, grow new teeth, they can. However, if you want to attract clients and develop a thriving practice, you might want to consider keeping those less-than-universal beliefs to yourself. At least, keep those beliefs confined within the circle of like minds in which you run.

It is a far, far better thing to be remembered by people because you gave them a fabulous and highly beneficial reading, and not because you looked and acted like something out of a Hollywood costume department, a traveling circus sideshow, or someone on the fringe of society.

*

In the business of being psychic, make it your business to be real.   You are meant to be a genuinely unique being. Intentionally being anything other than your most wonderful unique self is nothing short of weird.

CHAPTER 7:

YOUR COMPETITIVENESS

Healthy competition has a positive, purposeful, and rightful place in our lives, particularly when it gets our physical or creative juices flowing. In athletics, we compete with ourselves to achieve a personal best, and it's a basis for camaraderie in team sports. The healthy spirit of competition also rouses the warrior in us to kick an opponent's ass in Scrabble, Monopoly, or Balderdash! For children, scholastic competitions, such as science fairs and spelling bees, are venues to expand their minds. Competitiveness is healthy when the goal is to bring out the best of ourselves; it's not so healthy when the goal is to diminish, sabotage, or crush someone else. Unless it's a board game, then go for the jugular!

For a psychic, competitiveness is a great thing if it's used to stretch and improve one's own abilities, to achieve a "personal best." But being competitive with other psychics, with our spiritual brethren, is in no uncertain terms healthy—and in no uncertain terms is it spiritual.

When I started doing this work, I never dreamed that there could be such a dog-eat-dog mentality amongst those who were supposed to be in the biz of doing Spirit's work. I thought that attitude only existed in politics and in the corporate world—or so I thought. At least in those worlds, a person knows what they're walking into and can prepare accordingly. When there's rivalry in the metaphysical community, it's very disillusioning. We see that kind of behavior with the occasional spiritual practitioner who forgets—or just blatantly disregards—the contents and principles of the New Age books they so readily regurgitate from. They'll use catchphrases such as, "God will provide," "there's more than enough abundance for all of us," "ask and it is given," and "we are all one." Don't get me wrong, it's not the words I take issue with, for there's tremendous wisdom in those words. The issue is the lack of sincerity behind them. When those words get spewed in one breath, however eloquently, and in the next the spewer maligns a fellow practitioner, it's the ugly lie of competitiveness. Essentially, they're talking a lot of talk, but the talk isn't getting walked.

Believing in Universal truths like "don't wish ill on others," "we're all brothers and sisters in spirit," "we're all connected," isn't enough. We have to live like we KNOW those truths, and then, and only then, will we recognize that other psychics are our colleagues, they're not our competitors. If you're going to speak to your clients about the whole brotherly/sisterly love thing, then you should be practicing what you preach. You and I and all other spiritual practitioners are associates working for the same philanthropic organization, namely, Infinite Intelligence. We're working for a common cause, which is expanded consciousness on this planet, and there's always plenty of work for all of us. If you watch even a little bit of the news you'll see that we will never, ever, ever run out of work! As a matter of fact, we're in a time in history where each of us will have to put in a lot of overtime!! With that guarantee of job security, there's no need for competitiveness between us.

Competitiveness is a lie that our egos perpetuate. The truth is that we're each far too unique than to have to stoop to the low vibration of competitiveness with one another. Recognize our own uniqueness, see the uniqueness of your spiritual comrades, and you'll see that any competitiveness with other psychics is moot, and a non-truth.

There are countless ways to tap into Source, and we each tap in our own way. We each work with our clients using our own methods, our own tools, and our own distinct abilities. In other words, all of us unique ones do our own unique things, so it's unnecessary to compete with someone else's uniqueness!

Not being competitive also means that you're not envious of the abilities that other psychics possess. Most of us can tap into the energy of just about any aspect of someone's life, but some psychics are "specialists" in specific areas. These folks can "go deep" into those areas, deeper and more explicitly than the rest of us can. Let's touch on just a few.

Medical intuitives are the specialists for health readings. They have a broader knowledge—and many have some formal education—in physiology, anatomy, biochemistry, or diseases. They can go deep in that arena with their clients. Frankly, why would a client want a health reading from someone who doesn't know one sphincter from another? So, you see, there's no need for jealously when a client gets a reading from a specialist. Most of us can't compete with that—and we shouldn't want to. After all, having that specialized gift does come with a price. Medical intuitives deal with a lot of very sick individuals, and on more occasions than most of us can imagine, they have to be the bearer of bad news. Those aren't situations most of us would want to be in competition for.

Some psychics only do finances and investments. The consultations with their clients focus specifically on trading stocks, bonds, and commodities. There's a definite uniqueness about them in that they're a psychic that reads, understands, and discusses articles from *The Wall Street Journal* with their clientele. I bet it's safe to say, that's unlike most of us woo-woos! I'll be the first to admit that I can't make those right brain-left brain connections! I've known a couple of financial psychics that, in fact and dollars, had done pretty well for themselves in the market. But would most of us want to be competitive with them? Have you ever tried to read and/or comprehend the Wall Street Journal?! There's your answer!

Psychics who work with law enforcement are, in my opinion, the most unenviable of the specialists. It may appear exciting, and even glamorous, when there's media attention on their work; however, the public doesn't actually see what those psychics see, hear what they hear, or feel what they feel—and neither do any of us who won't go near that kind of low vibrational stuff. When they go deep they're immersing themselves in some pretty horrific energy that's imprinted in those crime scenes. They go deep into the twisted psyches of murderers, rapists, child molesters. If you've ever attempted to tap into that kind of energy field, you know what I'm talking about. One has to not only be called to do that kind of work but has to be unequivocally hard-wired to handle it. Unique doesn't even begin to describe them.

Then there are the animal communicators. In my opinion, they're not just unique, but they've also got it easy. Many of them strictly read for non-humans, and most of them will flat-out say that they prefer it that way since animals are much easier to read for than their people—that's because the animals don't argue! Still, their work is not to be envied. The critters' readings are predominately messages *for* and *about* their humans. So, as some clients do, they will oftentimes object to what they're being told. But I think that animal communicators have it easy because when the human starts to argue they can simply throw up their hands and tell the human, "Hey, go home and take it up with Fluffy!"

There will be times when the best thing you can do for your clients is refer them to a psychic specialist. Firstly, that will require being completely honest with yourself about your limitations, which, of course, means not letting ego get in the way so you can recognize that there's even a limitation. Next, you have to view it like you're sending them to a specialist and not to a competitor. For instance, perhaps your client needs to talk to their dearly departed Dad. They may need to know where he stashed the cash he won at the casino the night before he made his transition. A medium can do that, and if you're not a medium, the right thing to do is to refer them to one. Another situation would be where you have a client with a serious health issue who'd benefit from psychic diagnostics. If you're not a medical intuitive, refer them to one.

Personally, tapping into past lives is not my strong suit. When I do pick up on a particular past life, it's pretty much a generality. It's not my forte to go deep into my clients' previous lifetimes, and, frankly, it's not something I really even like to do—I guess I don't have the stomach to see the Vlad the Impaler life! So, if someone calls me asking specifically for a past life reading, I refer them to a colleague, a past life specialist. I know that she'll give them the specifics they're looking for—specifics I can't compete with.

Not being competitive also means that you're willing to suggest that a client get a second opinion should they have extraordinary circumstances or very complex decisions to make. That's not to say that your abilities are inadequate, it's just that every once in a blue moon, more information from a different angle is needed. In a case like that, another reader and their Guidance may be able to provide the client with a different set of particulars about their situation. A concurrent reading can also serve as a complimentary one, or a confirmation, to what the client had already gotten from you. When details overlap, it's validation for both psychics, but most importantly, additional validation and clarity for the client about their situation.

If a client's circumstance warrants a second opinion reading, it shouldn't be looked at as a competition or as dueling psychics. It's not a psychic "read-off!" Think of it as yin-yanging, or what I prefer to call it: tag-teaming—and the tagging is for Team Client. If your client is in an exceptionally challenging situation, or if they have a life-altering decision to make—which is when and why a client would need a psychic specialist or a second opinion—they'll benefit greatly from a tag-team. Know, too, that they'll appreciate that you had their well-being at heart.

So, instead of DIS-couraging clients from consulting with other psychics, they should be EN-couraged to consult with other psychics, if their circumstances warrant it. Have no doubt that that will reflect well on you, it will endear you to your clients, which will, in turn, be very favorable for your business.

But there is a flip side to that. When a client gets multiple readings on a matter, most often the readings will complement one another, yet sometimes that's not so. Conflicting messages about the same situation are not improbable, and predictions about the outcome to that situation can differ greatly. The reason for that, first and foremost, comes down to the variables, of course. Also, because there are no *absolutes* in a reading, and except for death, taxes, and vodka, there is no absolute anything in life.

When we tap into a client's energy field "du jour," we're merely seeing the *probabilities* at that moment in time and seeing what will happen if they stay their du jour course. Should they change their mind, they change their energy field, which can change everything. So, if two psychics read for the same person a day apart—or even an hour apart—they each will be reading a changed energy field. It's no wonder then that different readings can produce entirely different predictions—and not because the psychics were wrong. As an example, let's say that a woman goes to a psychic on a Friday afternoon seeking career guidance. In the reading the psychic sees a fabulous new job with a hefty salary, a brand-new luxury company car, a gorgeously decorated corner office, and lots of other perks. Even juicier, the psychic sees a handsome co-worker who would like to occupy her "after-hours!" The woman is amazed at the psychic's abilities because she just applied for a position exactly like that and said that she was hoping and praying with all her might to get it. The psychic then begins to tell the woman that she also sees that there's another opportunity for her, but the woman abruptly cuts her off. She is adamant that she wants the fabulous and prestigious job with all the trimmings, including Mr. Co-Worker-With-Benefits. The psychic tells her that it is hers. With that, the client leaves happy and thrilled out of her mind, thinking that she needs to go shopping for some new silky, lacey underwear.

Over the weekend this woman thinks about the new job and all the delicious accoutrements that go with it. And *him*. But then she begins to consider all the responsibility that she'll have to shoulder with the new position, and all the time she'll have to invest in it. It concerns her that she potentially won't even have time for *him*. But then she thinks, *forget him, hell, I need time for myself! Is he trying to monopolize my time?? Men are sooo like that, ya know!!* She does a lot of thinking, then on Monday afternoon she goes to see a different psychic for a reading. This psychic tells her that a new path is opening up for her. She's told that this endeavor doesn't pay much but it's very peaceful and will afford her plenty of time for contemplation.

A couple of weeks later, sure enough, the woman is offered that fabulous position—just as the first psychic predicted. But she turns it down. Instead, she has decided to leave behind the world she knows, join a convent, and take a vow of celibacy (the cost of new underwear was probably the deciding factor).

Was Psychic #1 wrong? No. The prediction came to pass. The fabulous job was offered to that woman. She just decided to pass on it. Was Psychic #2 better? No. Psychic #2 was no better and no more accurate than Psychic #1. Each psychic related the probability of the energy field they read. Both were accurate in reading the client's energy field "du jour."

We can see by that scenario that there's no reason to compare ourselves to other psychics or be competitive with our colleagues in this work. We can all be derailed by our clientele. Comforting, isn't it?

Finally, if you ever for even a nano-second believe you have to compete for business, let me assure you that there is an infinite amount of people with an infinite amount of problems on this planet who are in infinite need of guidance from Infinite Intelligence! *Oh pleeease*, there aren't enough of us to accommodate all of them!! See for yourself, just watch the news! On second thought, don't do that.

If you are a good psychic working in integrity, keeping your vibration high, and focusing on being the best *you* can be, you will always have clientele. And, as an aside, you'll also have lots of friends and love in your life, because that's just a damned good way to be and people will flock to you! They might actually compete for your attention!!

*

In the business of being psychic, the only place for competitiveness is nowhere to be found in your business.

CHAPTER 8:

YOUR SPACE

Your space, the setting in which you do your thing, the place you invite your clients and summon your Guidance, is a physical representation of who you are. It doesn't matter whether you rent an office in a commercial building or have a room in your home, what matters is that your space makes a clear statement that you're a professional who takes pride in the work you do and the service that you provide.

If you're just beginning to set up a new space or rearranging the current one, hold everything! Before hanging a picture, laying down a rug, moving your table, or buying a new inflatable spaceship, do what's most important: think. Think about how you want your clients to perceive you. Think about what kind of first impression you wish to make. Think about what kind of lasting impression that you want your clients to leave with. Think about what a client will tell other people—a.k.a., potential clients—about you and their experience with you. You may be a remarkably gifted psychic, but have no doubt that your physical environment will be a huge factor in how the reading is judged overall. When your space makes a favorable impression on clients, they will come back to see you, and they will refer other people to you. A space that makes an unfavorable impression can overshadow your abilities and misrepresent who you are. Your space matters.

Above all else, your space needs to be clean. A little dusting and a quick vacuuming goes a long way in how a client reacts to and feels in your space. Long before a client arrives, make sure that there's a clear and uncluttered path to where you're conducting the session. Pick up anything a person could trip over—you want clients to fall for you, but not in that way! Your table or desk should be cleared off and ready for the reading. If you use your table for anything other than readings, it's not only impolite, it's highly unprofessional to expect your client to sit there and wait for you to clear off your breakfast plates, a pile of newspapers, soiled diapers, or the jigsaw puzzle you've been working on. And make sure the chair they're to be seated on is clean. When your client leaves your space, they should only take with them the brilliant and useful messages they got in the reading—not food stains or cat hair stuck on their backside!

Once the space is picked up enough for company, which is a good standard we can all understand, use all your senses to objectively critique it. The best way to do that is to step outside the area momentarily and then step back in. Imagine yourself as being a first-time client that's coming to see you. With that in mind, impersonally evaluate your space. And remember, you only have one chance to make a good first impression.

As you walk into your space, ask yourself what the initial visual impression is. Ideally, it should be relatively neutral. That, in no way, means it has to be boring! What it means is that it's not being over the top in the décor, i.e., in theme (aliens), in furnishings (a velvet throne), or in color (purple everything and purple everywhere). Neutral is playing it safe, yes, but remember, safe is the way you want your clients to feel with you. Neutral is inviting because it feels familiar and reliable, which makes people comfortable. So what constitutes neutral? Well, it certainly doesn't dictate that the only paint color you're allowed to use is beige— unless, of course, your favorite color is beige, then by all means, beige-away! It also doesn't mean that the only artwork adorning your walls is pastel flowers. Oh, heaven's no! Color is absolutely encouraged. Using the right colors can bring life into the environment, they can sooth emotions, they can be subliminally inviting, and above all, colors will affect the vibration of the space.

On the contrary, colors can also be repulsing. That's why it's so important to be sensitive about what colors you use, and then temper *how much* of those colors you're using. A tone that's loud and garish will feel anything but soothing and inviting to your clients; anything too dark might give them the creeps. Let's take black, for example. I love black. It's a great color (technically, though, it's a lack of color). I wear a lot of black; after all, it goes with everything, it's slimming, and it hides stains caused by my sloppy eating. But I wouldn't even dream of painting my space black. Again, looking through the eyes of a client, it would give a subliminal impression that I was trying to hide, or "blacken out," my space or something about myself. Besides, it would just look plain creepy.

As far as what's hanging on the walls, a word to the wise: don't offend. There are some images that will undoubtedly elicit very strong negative emotions in your average client. Among them are swastikas, the Confederate flag, an inverted pentagram, pornographic images—even if they're done in watercolor. You get the picture?

Neutral doesn't just apply to the colors you use and artwork you have. When it comes to your political views, neutrality in your space is your friend and your best business partner. Whether you're a blue, a red, a green, or a purple, in your work space it will be in your best interest to be a beige or a gray (all fifty shades if you like...). In other words, keep a lid on your personal politics—particularly during big elections! Aside from religion, there are few other subject matters that can bring out the worst of the worst in folks. That's especially true for people who are in lock-step with their political party. They'd be the rabid ones who take a *"if you're not with us, you're a-gin us"* attitude! Think about that. If you have a political sign out for your clients to see, you have a fifty-fifty chance of being an "a-gin us!"

You may feel very passionate about politics and about your particular candidate or political party. Maybe you're even one of those rabids (in that case, I apologize if I offend). You may also enjoy having a good debate. That's all fine and good. However, your space is not the arena for debating politics. It's supposed to be a place where Spirit flows—and Spirit doesn't flow anywhere near political dogma and division! If you get into a heated debate with a client, you risk losing that client. Yes, you might prove victorious in the debate, and you may feel ever so righteous because you made the sacrifice of losing a client. But, really, do you think that that's going to help your candidate win or get your ballot issues passed? Absolutely not. Frankly, for you, it's a lose-lose situation. Of course, it's your space, and you can do whatever you want to in it. But if you want to build your business, you'll save your disputations for an appropriate time and place, like in a bar......with your pals.......drinking way too much alcohol. Ya know, having a good time.

And then there's that other hot topic of religion. It's a sad fact, but when it comes to our spiritual beliefs, being a hair past neutral can get you branded as a heathen, a witch, or even a Satan worshiper—if you just get called a weirdo, you're lucky! Be mindful of that when it comes to your work space. The intention is for your clients to feel comfortable. Let's be honest here, those of us who embrace the occult or are metaphysically-inclined can go a *wee* little bit overboard in trying to make a space seem other worldly—and other worldly is fine as long as the world isn't so far out there that it freaks out your clients.

The objective is to attract a broad range, or mainstream, clientele. To do that, we have to tone down the woo-woo. Before covering every bit of your wall space with pentacles, ankhs, deities with animal heads, spaceships, or having a candle burning for every saint that was ever canonized, stop and reconsider. It's not that you can't have any of those things in your space. You can and should. Personally, I wouldn't consider not having Ganesh, Archangel Michael, and St. Jude in my office! Just don't go overboard. The people who are coming to see us hope that we can relate to them; conversely, it helps if they can relate to us, as well. Our space is where we can make or break those relate-abilities. So, everything in moderation, especially with idols and effigies.

If you share space with others, being neutral takes on even more importance. To say that each occupant who uses the space needs to feel comfortable working in it, is a given. But, equally important, is that each occupant needs to feel that they're represented by, and that they have their own fingerprint on, the space. Depending on the people involved, that's what can prove to be somewhat of a challenge.

Once, and only once, I rented an office with another psychic. It was a low-rent for a low-budget deal, and we had to provide our own signage. My office partner suggested that we commission an artist friend of hers to do our sign. She liked the artist personally; she said that he was a very talented professional and, even better, we'd get a good deal since they were friends. Being as how I'm all about delegating, as well as getting a good deal, I said, "Great, go ahead and have him do it."

Well, being lazy and cheap didn't work out for me. I walked in one day to find a Mickey Mouse sign on our front door. I don't mean mickey mouse as in unprofessional or tacky (but, yeah, it was that too). I literally mean it was Mickey the Mouse himself. The sign had Mickey dressed up as a wizard with our names *magically* appearing under his wand. Now, I admit to being a big fan of the Mickey—along with Minnie, Goofy, Pluto, and the rest of the gang—but I was not comfortable with Mickey being the face of my business. Or being my front man—I mean, mouse.

Mickey Mouse was my clients' first impression of me. I recognize fully that Mickey Mouse pushed my insecurity and my self-worth buttons (hmmm, it's not every day you hear someone say that, is it?!). Obviously, the other psychic didn't have my issues because she thought it was cute. Nevertheless, two parties occupied that space and one of them was never happy with that sign. I never did say anything though. I guess I was a bit mousy about it. The point is, whether it's beliefs, colors, political viewpoints, or cartoon characters, shared space needs to be a neutral zone.

Where there's no place for neutrality is in your commitment to making your space as dedicated to your work as you possibly can—or at least give it that appearance. If your clients come to see you in your home, your workspace should look like your workspace, and not like a hurriedly cleared out corner of the junk room. Even if square-footage in the home is limited, in almost any case it's not impossible to create a cozy little nook. You may not have the luxury of having a room to call completely your own, so consider setting up an area in a guest room, a study, or even a walk-in closet. The kitchen or dining room are also options, as long as you clear out the family and any dirty dishes! No matter the logistics, with some ingenuity and with a few easy decorating tricks, i.e., a little paint, some curtains, a room dividing screen, and tidiness, it can look like a dedicated space. And, most significantly, it will feel that way to your clients.

Being dedicated also means that privacy is ensured. Your clients need to feel a strong sense of security when they're working with you. If they don't, they won't come back to you. Therefore, know that you have a responsibility to them—and to growing your business—to take every possible measure you can to create that sacred place of trust. An airtight container, so to speak, in which whatever you, your client, and Infinite Intelligence, discusses in the session will not be overheard by anyone else. If you work from home, you might think about putting a Do Not Disturb sign on the door. It's amazing how effective those signs can be—particularly when you threaten bodily harm to anyone who doesn't abide by it!

Absolute privacy may be a bit of a challenge if you share office space with other people. One of the better arrangements would be to assign each person their own day in the office. Or even specific hours. For instance, whoever likes mornings, gets the mornings, while those who prefer evenings, get evenings. At the very least, agree to check in with each other before booking appointments. And if checking in with each other is the agreement you all have, then ALL PARTIES had better be good at communicating! If not, mix-ups can happen very easily and very often—especially during Mercury Retrogrades!!

Another thing to survey in your space is the flow of it. If it's cramped, if it's cluttered, or if the arrangement just feels off, it's something to remedy. It's more than just being concerned about the aesthetics or the poor impression you're giving your clients. Any of those can cause the energy of the space—the Chi—to get blocked, which means blocked energy for your business. Essentially, that's a big clog in your energetic pipes, which blocks the flow of business, the flow of clients, and the flow of dollars.

After cleaning up, if you still can't seem to get a good flow of energy going in your space, Feng Shui just may be the remedy—the remedies, as they're called. To find a good, bona fide Feng Shui consultant in your area, your best bet will be your local metaphysical store. The stores tend to be the hub for metaphysicians and alternative practitioners, so if there's a Feng Shui person to be found in your area, they'll know about them. But reputable practitioners aren't a dime-a-dozen, so there's a chance that one may not be in your area. If that's the case, an online search will surely find one that you'll resonant with. Just like with readings, it's not necessary for the Feng Shui consultation to be done in-person or on location. You can work effectively—and very successfully—with someone by telephone or through email.

Then again, maybe you're a do-it-yourselfer. If that's how you roll, get a good, easy-to-follow book on the art. Actually, before you go out or go online and buy a new book, you may want to check your bookshelf. Prospects are good that you'll find that you already have a book—I mean, don't we all?! That's especially true for those of us who remember when Feng Shui was "trendy!" So, either buy one or dust off the one on your shelf and get Feng Shui-ing!

If you're not familiar with it—and that would only be if you're not old enough to remember the trend—I can attest that the remedies are incredibly simple and inexpensive. Things such as eliminating clutter, making a minor tweak in furniture arrangement, placing a little mirror here and there, putting flowers in a particular spot, or some other very doable things. Truly, very simple little things, but it's crazy how those little things can make a world of difference in moving the energy in or out of a space. And when Chi moves, hello clients!

Once you've established how you want your space to be, it's time to establish how you're going to **be** in your space. What I mean is, establish your protocol for how you're going to meet and treat your clientele. The best advice I can share, and as cliché as it sounds, is: put yourself in your clients' shoes and treat them as you would like to be treated. Here are a few things I'd recommend:

Greeting

Making your clients feel welcomed in your space, begins by actually welcoming your clients into your space. How you welcome them—or don't welcome them—will set the tone for the session. Just like when we invite guests to our home it's customary to greet them at the door and welcome them in, right? Well, your clients are your guests and should be treated as such. When they knock, go to the door and open it. Don't holler at them from inside, *"Come on in, the door's open."* If your door is already open and you're sitting at your desk—even if your desk is only five feet away from the door—don't just wave them in. Get up, greet them with a hand shake or a hug, and usher them in. Direct them to their seat. If it's convenient, offer them something to drink, like a bottle of water. Make your clients feel welcome in your space.

Ease Anxiety

Beyond common courtesy, a warm greeting will put your client at ease. Keep in mind that it's not unusual for people to feel anxious when coming for a reading. If they're a virgin and it's their first time, being nervous is almost guaranteed. But even the clients who check in regularly might still be a bit nervous. As we well know, their apprehension isn't without some basis. Good grief, neither they nor we ever know what messages Spirit has in store for him or her! So, a warm hello and a smile at the doorway can go a very long way to soothe their nerves. Doing these seemingly insignificant things to make your clients feel comfortable will pave the way for a great session—and for those clients to return.

Eliminate Distractions

Making certain that you'll be as distraction-less as humanly possible also assures a great session. Some distractions are unavoidable. It could be the guy in the next office who could benefit (his employees would benefit more) from anger management, or it's an impromptu fire drill in the building, or street traffic. Or it's even possible that there's a psychic down the hall who laughs too loud......I'm told. You can't control everything. All you can do at those times is look over at your client, shrug your shoulders—and laugh! However, there are other distractions that are completely in our control.

I have to start this by saying, I LOVE DOGS! I LOVE DOGS! I LOVE, LOVE, LOVE DOGS!! And, personally, I can't imagine my life without a pack—or not having dog hair on my clothes! However, not everyone feels the same way. If you work from home and you have dogs, it may pose an issue. As I said earlier, when your clients come to your door they should be greeted, but their greeting shouldn't include being jumped on by your dogs. Even those folks that are dog lovers shouldn't be subjected to having their clothes covered with your dog's hair, muddied with paw prints, or slobbered on.

If you, like Caesar Milan, are a dog whisperer, then there's no problem. Your dogs will stay in their places and your clients won't even know they're there. If that's the case, feel free to skip over the next couple of paragraphs. On the other hand, if you're like the rest of us, asking your fur-babies to refrain from meeting and greeting company is just too much to ask of them!! After all, they're convinced that anyone who walks through the door is solely there to visit and play with them. But if you want clientele, you'll have to step into alpha-mode and claim your territory—albeit temporarily.

When you have appointments, put the pups in another room with a chewy, their favorite toy, and some classical music or DogTV. Otherwise, and only when weather permits, they can go outside to play or nap in the back yard. This accomplishes two things in the order of their importance: 1. your pups will be content; and, 2. they won't be disruptive to the session.

Personally, I can't have clients come to my home. All I can do are phone readings. Even then, before I get on a call I have to give my darlings a bribe......I mean a treat....so they'll be quiet—unless they hear the UPS truck, or FedEx, or anyone who dares walk down their street. But all the treats in the world wouldn't work if I had **PEOPLE!** (translation: new friends and admirers) come to my house. Not even remotely being the dog whisperer, I just pay to rent an office fifteen miles away. That's a fair arrangement, don't you think?

There are a couple of exceptions though. The first exception is a no-brainer and that would be if you required a therapy dog. In that case, there's no refuting that your dog stays with you. These K-9 buddies are well-trained and wouldn't be disruptive in the least. That being said, you very well may encounter a distraction problem anyway—and it won't be on the part of your dog. Be prepared to "train" your clients to pay attention to you and to leave your dog alone! If you have a therapy dog, you know exactly what I'm talking about!! It's just like when these dogs are out in public wearing the vest that clearly identifies them as an on-duty therapy dog, some people just don't get it. That vest, it seems, is a magnet for oohs and awws and "may I pet your dog?" I always feel so stupid when I get a harsh "no" and a dirty look.

The other exception would be if you have elderly dogs. Geriatric pups usually don't care if someone is in their home. And if they're very geriatric, sadly, they may not even know that someone is in their home. What's even sadder is that the *really* geriatric don't know that they're home! In those cases, let sleeping dogs lay.

Cats in your space can present even more of an issue for your clientele. First of all, an extraordinary number of people are allergic to cat dander. Also, cats tend to jump up on everything and everyone. Remember *confirmation kitties*?! If you have cats jumping up and around on everything and everyone, all that you'll be confirming is loss of clientele! Just like your dogs, during consultations your feline friends should be relegated to one of their happy places. Most likely it's a sunny room with a great view of the birdfeeders. Put them wherever they're content to be—along with their cleaned-out litter boxes. Litter boxes should be as far away as possible from your work space and kept absolutely clean. Of course, keeping them clean is a good policy in general. Seriously, cat box smell stinks!

If you have children, the ideal thing to do for everyone's sake would be to schedule your appointments either during school hours or, for the real little ones, when the kiddos are down for a long and, what you're sure will be, uninterrupted nap. Otherwise, try to get a neighbor, a friend, or hire a baby-sitter to watch them for an hour or so. If you need an entire day because you have back-to-back appointments, maybe their grandma or grandpa would like to take them for an outing. Face it, regardless of how young or old they are, kids will be kids, and it's very likely that the time with your client will be interrupted.

Now, I get it, I'm a bit anal about distractions, and you may think that I'm unrealistic about the measures I suggest to avoid them. But this is about having a successful business. Be anal because you're a professional with whom a client has made an appointment, and the client will be compensating you for a specified amount of dedicated time. Not only will they compensate you, but recognize that they had to block out that amount of time from their own schedule to meet with you. Their time should be valued. Also, ask yourself, if you were the client, would you want the time you've scheduled and are paying for to be intruded upon? Do you see the point of my anal-ness—and why you should be a bit anal too?

Stuff happens, but aside from an unexpected emergency, or an act of God, like, let's say, a tsunami, an asteroid hit, or a pole shift (we are close to the 26,000-year mark), nothing and no one should interrupt or infringe on the time with your clients. There should be no crying babies, no barking dogs, no blaring televisions, or no phones ringing. If you have housemates, ask and/or bribe them to be as quiet as they can be. Seriously, don't dismiss bribery, it's a very powerful tool!

There's one distraction that will walk in with your client, and you'd be wise to put a stop to it before it starts ringing, and that's their cell phone—and you definitely want to put the kibosh on them answering it! To say the least, it's annoying. Their phone begins to ring and then they're fumbling around trying to find it to turn it off, if you're lucky. Some clients will actually take the call—and it's not like they have to take it because they're on the organ transplant recipient list! It's just rude. Let me tell you, though, if you keep the timer going and their conversation comes out of their session time, they'll get the message really quick!

But there's an easier way to get your clients to turn off their cell phones. At the beginning of the session, point to the big sign on your table that reads, **"FOR GOD'S SAKE, TURN OFF YOUR CELL PHONE!"** Nooo, I'm just kidding. A small sign will do. Really though, a subtle, yet very effective way is to have your own phone in your hand as you sit down. Then, as you proceed to turn your phone off, say to your client, "You're here now so I'll turn off my phone so we're not interrupted." They will follow your lead. It works every time. Unless they are, indeed, waiting for the call about their new organ. I'd turn the timer off for that.

Ambiance and Comfort

Let's talk sound. Still pretending you're a client, be very still and take a listen. What do you hear? Nothing? Perfect! It doesn't have to be absolutely silent, however. Having some New Age or classical music, or soothing sounds like ocean waves or bells, playing softly in the background is great for ambiance, as well as for raising the vibration of the space. Blaring music, no matter what kind it is, is discouraged. First of all, it doesn't lend to an intimate setting, which is needed to talk to clients. Also, it's not conducive to tuning into other realms to communicate messages. Even if you have no trouble tuning in regardless of the volume, your client **will** have trouble hearing you. *Anything* blaring, whether it's Tibetan bowls, chanting monks, a babbling brook, can be assaulting to the ears and nerves. Bear in mind that some of the messages that your clients hear from Infinite Wisdom will feel like assaults to their ears—because sometimes the truth hurts! Although you can't control how they're going to interpret their messages, you do have control over the music volume knob. So, turn it to way down soft and low.

I would also like to make one other suggestion with respect to music, and that is that you try to avoid music with lyrics—the exception is Enya, because nobody knows what she's singing half the time, so it doesn't matter. Why no *understandable* lyrics? Because it's always a possibility that a client may have just broken up with someone when they come to see you. If by chance the music you're playing is "their song," or some other heart-wrenching break-up song, it can be utterly devastating to them. Think about that. Haven't we all at some time—or many times—in our lives known that wretched feeling? Have you ever freshly broken up with someone and heard Whitney Houston or Dolly Parton singing, *I Will Always Love You*? Talk about having your heart ripped out and stomped on! Oh, and that reminds me, it's a good idea to keep a few extra boxes of facial tissues on hand.

Next up, walk outside and take a couple of breaths of fresh air to clear your sinuses. Come back in and then, still acting as if you are a client, take a big whiff. If there is any smell whatsoever, it should be pleasant, soft, and faint—with the emphasis on faint. If you detected the scent before you got back inside—or saw a cloud of smoke—I'd say it's probably a tad bit much.

It's a scientific fact that smell has an effect on us, and there's no question that the right scent, or blend of scents, can be a great little ally for a reading. A little aromatherapy in the form of a mildly scented candle, a wax or oil burner, or a good quality incense can help quiet a client's conscious mind, sooth their emotions, and relax their body—and yours, if you have a very trying client! Using some ylang-ylang or geranium can help put a fearful or traumatized client into a calm and receptive state. And I don't know about you, but that's how I prefer my clients—makes my job so much easier! Just keep in mind that when you're using scent in your space, it's best to follow the "less is more" rule.

But even with the best intentions and a keen nose, I have to add this caveat about using aromatherapy. In spite of the benefits, every now and then you'll have a client who has scent allergies. Talk about something messing up a perfectly good reading! I mean, the client is rubbing their eyes, they'll have tears running down their face, they're choking, their face swells up—and you're thinking that they're reacting to your brilliance, but then they whip out their EpiPen and inject themselves! I jest a little. Actually, I never had anyone swell up or need an EpiPen, but one time I did have a client react to the incense I was burning. It was at her unfortunate expense that I learned about scent allergies. After that experience, I made it a practice to ask clients as soon as they arrive if the scent bothers them. If it does, I make a note to self and then plan accordingly for their next session—which means being scents-less. You might want to adopt that practice.

Scent allergy or not, above all else, make sure there are no unpleasant smells, like cat boxes—yes, I've got a little PTSD associated with cat boxes! Just to be sure, recruit a friend or family member with unbiased nostrils to come by for, shall we say, a breather.

With sight, sound, and smell checked off the list, the easy stuff is done! What will need to be done in your space constantly and consistently is clearing the energy, clearing the energy, clearing the energy, and more clearing the energy!! Energy will stick to your space like white on rice. That's not surprising when you consider that you're bringing in many different people with all their many different problems and issues and emotions and dramas and traumas. And that's not all. It's compounded by your own energy, that of your family, and all other energies that walk through your door. Lord knows, with all of that stuff, something's gonna stick—and it's usually the noxious entities and energies! Ya gotta clear it!!

It doesn't matter how you clear the energy, it just matters that you **do** clear it and clear it regularly. Use whatever means works best for you, whatever you've been taught to do or use, or whatever you're comfortable working with. Burn some sage, sprinkle sea salt or holy water, ring bells, spray essential oils, call in your angels, or use whatever you wield most powerfully. Likening it to how we clean our floors, everyone has their preferred method. Some people prefer to sweep with a broom, some to push a vacuum cleaner around, others like to use a dust mop, and some of us would rather watch the iRobot Roomba do its thing. The instrument doesn't matter. The important thing is to set your intention to clear your space, take your tool of choice, and just do it—often.

So how does your space *feel* to you? You're a psychic, so this should be easy! Does it *feel* light? Does it *feel* comfortable? Those are the *feelings* you want to achieve and maintain. Whether or not you can see heavy or dark energy, you will, without question, be able to feel it. And if you do, it's time to clear it out. Frankly, if you're feeling heaviness, it's past time, so you'd better get on it! There's no getting around it, we have to energetically clear our space just as often as we dust and vacuum our homes. Actually, that may not be a good example, because *some* of us should dust and vacuum at least as much as we clear the energy (I'm holding my hand up). It's a chore, certainly, but if you think it's a chore that you can skimp on (after all, you can't see energy like you can see filth and clutter), think again. If you don't do this chore religiously—and take that literally or figuratively—after a very short while your clientele will begin to feel it. They may not be able to pinpoint exactly what it is they're feeling, but they'll know it doesn't feel good, and they won't feel comfortable in your space.

There will be times when an energy comes in and doesn't want to leave. It can be anything from an innocuous lost or confused soul to a dark and potentially malicious entity. It may stick around because it likes you and thinks you're cute or it may want to annoy you, at the very least, or wreak some serious havoc. Whatever or whoever it is, you might have trouble clearing it out on your own. *So, who ya gonna call? Ghost Busters!* Sorry, I couldn't resist that. But I'm only half-kidding. It would be to your advantage to develop a working and/or reciprocal relationship with a good energy worker in your area. If you currently don't know anyone, as is always my advice, head to your local metaphysical store. Chances are that they'll be able to recommend someone who is good at clearing out, collapsing, or sending away difficult energies.

Personally, I'm blessed to have an extraordinary energy worker to collaborate with. I turn to her for help to clean up my occasional sticky-icky situations when my sage isn't doing it. What's more, it's an advantage to be able to refer my clients to her that have "unwanted visitors." I honestly don't know what she does, but I do know that she blends several modalities, along with her own abilities, and she's a formidable force. She knows what I need when I call and ask to speak to the Warrior Princess! She's someone who can clear out a room fast—and I mean that in a good way!!

To ask for or call on help from another professional doesn't make any one of us less of a spiritual worker. That's what they do, that's their expertise, that's the work they signed up to do when they came here—they're the specialists. So, if you can't fend off the more difficult or stubborn energies, call someone. You don't have to be your own ghost buster! And, for crying out loud, don't wait to call until things are flying across the room—or worse—before you call in a professional!

Lastly,

Bid Adieu

When the reading is over, thank your client for coming in and allowing you to be a part of their life journey. If it was a particularly emotionally session, and if you have the time, give them a few extra minutes to collect themselves before sending them on their way. Then walk them to the door and, if appropriate, offer them a hug—and accept a hug back. You deserve it.

When you walk into your space, it should bring a smile to your face (ha, I made a rhyme!). It should reflect to others that you take what you do seriously and you take great pride in doing it. Your space should make your clients feel welcome, comfortable, secure, and above all, glad they came to see you.

In the business of being psychic, get a sense of your space using all your senses. Keep it clean and clear because it's the container that holds your sessions—and keep it as sacred as the work you're doing.

CHAPTER 9:

YOUR WELL-BEING

Our business is practically the same as any other, with the *minor* exceptions of working with vibrational energies, tapping into different dimensions, and talking to non-physical beings—other than those things, it's no different. And just like anyone else who runs their own business, the well-being of body, mind, and spirit must be a priority in order to run the business. I believe this is the most important chapter of this book.

Let's begin with the well-being of the body. I'm not original here when I say that we're spiritual beings having a human experience; and since the human experience means inhabiting a human body, attention and care of that body is required. Sometimes spiritually-inclined folks have to be reminded of that because they spend an inordinate amount of their time and energy on their higher consciousness to the detriment of their physical selves. In other words, they spend most of their time focusing on their upper chakras and forget about the lower ones, or what the lower chakras govern, which is their physicality. A human who loses touch with their physicality makes for one very imbalanced being. So, folks, let's talk candidly about our physicality, shall we?

Our cars aren't the only vehicles that require maintenance. We sometimes forget that our physical bodies are also vehicles: the vehicles that carry the mind and the spirit. In that forgetting many of us drive our physical selves way harder than we would even think about driving our cars. We push our bodies harder than those times when we drive like a bat out of hell whenever there aren't any cops around! When something is driven really hard and for really long distances, upkeep is mandatory. Psychic work, besides life in general, can push the body to its limits, affecting health.

How is your physical well-being? Do you practice good health habits? Grandmothers have been saying it forever: *without your health, Dear, you have nothing*! Grandmas know. One of the other truths that grandmas give us is: *when I talk to you it goes in one ear and out the other!* I believe many of us are guilty of that. We tend not to give too much thought to our health until we become ill, get hurt, or drive ourselves so hard that we crash and burn. If we did stay tuned into—and get tune-ups for—the physical vehicle, we'd see that it pays off. Not only does that ensure that we have a fantabulous here-and-now human experience, but it affords us the heartiness and stamina to be able to do this work.   Thank you, Grandmas!

I've taken a lot of metaphysical classes in my day and rarely, if ever, was the impact on the physical body ever discussed—and the body is HUGELY impacted when we do this work. How could it not be? We're working in and with many different energies, mostly good, some maybe not so good, as well as operating in other realms and on different frequencies. If all that wasn't enough, we're dealing with people—and all of what that means! Good grief, add all those factors together and the body will feel as if it put in a full day of hard manual labor outdoors in the summertime in Phoenix!   In short, completely wiped out!! There's no getting around what you have to deal with, but by maintaining your health as best you can you will minimize the effects on your body. Of course, protecting yourself energetically is essential, but hand-in-hand with that, is keeping your physical body well.

Diet, exercise, and yeah, yeah, yeah, I hear you, tell you something you don't already know! Well, frankly, I can't. I can regurgitate what you already know, and that's that when we take care of ourselves we feel great, we have vitality, and we can fend off illness. But I can add something more specific, and that's that it helps a Lightworker to have good health in order to be able to navigate through all the various and sundry vibrational disturbances that are routinely encountered.

In the matter of health, professional psychics also need to consider how their clientele perceives them. More accurately, how clientele judge us. Whether they do it consciously or subconsciously, whether fairly or unfairly, whether they admit it or deny it, whether right or wrong, if they're a breathing human being, they're going to make a judgment. And one of the first things they'll judge is whether or not you reflect well-being.

Accepting that a judgment is going be made about us gives us the advantage to influence it. We can argue that we're merely the deliverers of the client's messages, but based on what they see before them, our clientele will judge whether we're a credible source *or not* for those messages. We can also argue that the messages come through us and not from us, but the fact is that our clients aren't just looking to us for guidance, they're also looking at us. They look at the person who is sitting in front of them, and they're looking through very human eyes, which will direct the brain to form an opinion. Knowing that, shouldn't we make it a point to present the healthiest possible picture of ourselves in their eyes?

To illustrate my point, let's pretend that you're seeking nutritional advice and, of course, you turn to Google, which tells you that there's a nutritionist nearby. When you get to the office you see a morbidly obese individual sitting there who reeks of barbecue potato chips, Slim Jims, and beer—yes, we're judging. Your thought might be, as my thought *would* be, that it's a good thing that this guy is getting the help he needs. But then the big guy introduces himself as the nutritionist.

Now, with that visual in your mind, ask yourself this question: "Myself (or whatever term of endearment you have for you), would I take diet and exercise advice from this person?" If you answer honestly, you'd probably say, "Are you freaking kidding?" or something very similar to that. Yet, this individual who's giving you this advice may have a top-notch education and be exceptionally knowledgeable. He may provide you with the best healthy eating tips you've ever gotten in your entire life. He may customize the most sound and doable exercise regimen you've EVER seen. BUT. And it's a big but (not just a big butt). Although logically you're well aware that he is only the messenger, his appearance (and aroma), does not lend to his credibility. And chances are, that's what you'll take away from your consultation with him.

Or, here's another example: Let's say that you're a smoker and you go see your doctor for a checkup. Then, during the exam your doctor begins to lecture you on the dangers of smoking, and she presents a strong and very convincing case to you to quit. Since you'd been thinking for quite a while that you should quit, you take her warning as a sign. But what if she smelled of cigarette smoke and had a pack of cigarettes poking out of her lab coat pocket? Even if her words and the facts that she presented had you convinced to quit, on some level you would find it difficult to take seriously the advice coming out of her mouth. Whether you were aware of it or not, you probably would've thought, "You're one to preach, lady!" And her messenger status would be not-at-all credible.

You're not going to see a rotund personal trainer with a lot of clients in the gym. You won't find a dentist with a mouthful of decayed or missing teeth with a booming practice. And a hairstylist with dirty, over-processed, chopped up hair? Forget about it. Most of us are too picky about who we entrust our manes to—unless dirty and chopped up is the newest trend in hairstyles! You get the picture. Then picture how you're perceived—and how you wish to be perceived—by your own clientele. Professional psychics need to take to heart the expression, "consider the source," because our clients do.

Let me be very clear here, in no way do I mean that to be a professional psychic you have to be a squeaky-clean, picture-perfect, goody-two-shoes, health fanatic! One doesn't have to go to extremes to maintain well-being. You don't need to be a bodybuilder, a marathoner, a yogi, or an Olympian. Nor is it mandated that you have to be a vegan, have to eat strictly organic and raw foods, or go sugarless (oh, my, no, no, no!). It's none of that. It's about being as healthy as possible in order to feel as good as possible. And we gotta admit that feeling our best feels really good—and feeling really good means looking our best! And it's really good when clients see us at our best!!

When you're at your best, your clients see a credible messenger for any health advice—or alerts—you channel for them. In that channeling, keep an ear open to what comes through. Although you probably know it already, just consider this to be a reminder: when messages come through for our clients, oftentimes the messages are also meant for us.

Divine Intelligence will use other people—specifically and especially our clients—to get whatever messages to us that we need to hear. If you pay attention, you'll see an ongoing theme, meaning that you'll have client after client after client with a similar problem or issue, and you'll be repeating the same warnings or guidance over and over again. Since there are no coincidences, you may just want to sit up and take heed—or you can keep doing similar readings and giving similar advice and wait for the inevitable two-by-four to hit you in the head!

One more thing with respect to the physicality factor. For this I wanna talk dirty to you. Actually, I want to talk *about* being dirty, i.e., not practicing good hygiene. Indeed, this is a very delicate and personal matter, but I would be remiss if I didn't address it. When you're dealing with people face-to-face, up close and in person, you really have to practice good hygiene—please! These physical bodies we occupy are carbon-based and, therefore, require proper care and cleaning. Brush your teeth, wash, or at least comb, your hair, bathe your body, and put on clean clothes. If you're going to wear flip-flops, at least be sure to have clean, groomed feet. By groomed I don't mean you have to get a pedicure. I'm referring to basic grooming practices, like clipping your toenails, and cleaning under the nails and between the toes. Get the picture? At the beginning of this book I said I would be drawing on personal experiences and, unfortunately, I'm drawing on more than a few personal encounters of the most unpleasant kind. I won't recount any of those experiences in great detail because some are just too......well......let's just say hard on the senses!

When you're at home, or in your office, but your only interaction with clients is via telephone or email, by all means go ahead and forgo the soap, toothpaste, deodorant, and toenail clippers (although your housemates may object!). If you're doing Skype, spiffy yourself a little bit from the waist up. You don't have to go all out, just put on a clean shirt and run a brush through your hair—or put on a hat! When your clients can't see you, or bluntly, can't smell you, feel free to be au natural!!

Being that friend—that most annoying friend—who points out that you have broccoli in your teeth, let me remind you that this is a business. If you currently work, or have worked in the past, for a corporation, you're expected to maintain certain hygienic and dress standards. Well, this is YOUR business. Because it is your business you have the luxury of being as comfortable as you wish to be. However, being comfortable doesn't mean you waive the shower or wear dirty, tattered, or odorous clothing. Of course, you can if you choose to, but you won't attract clients that way. Flies yes, a steady clientele, no.

When you make the effort to present yourself as a professional—a clean, fresh-scented one—your clients will view you, and will respect you, as a professional.

Another important component of a spiritual practitioner's well-being is having strong energetic boundaries. In this area, some of us have had to learn the hard way—and some of us are still trying to learn it! For most of us, this is something that can be quite a challenge, and it's easy to see why. When we work with clientele we walk a very fine energetic line. On one side of that line there's the necessary proximity to our clientele—and I don't mean in sitting together. We've got to be closely engaged with them—energetically, mentally, emotionally—in order to be effective; on the other side, we also have to be able to remain detached from their energy so we don't take any of it on ourselves. So, like I said, it's not always easy to do. But do we must; otherwise, our own energetic well-being suffers.

Now, if that wasn't enough, we also have to hold our boundaries from the energies our clients inevitably drag in. Certainly no one comes in with the intention of depositing their energetic cooties onto you or into your space. As a matter of fact, most people don't even know they have cooties! But they do—actually, we all do occasionally!! Hell, just by being human we're prone to be energetic cootie carriers! Just like fleas that hop from one animal to another, energetic cooties ride along on a host until they hop onto the next warm energy field. Until energetic cootie collars, spray, or powder is invented we'll just have to maintain strong and solid boundaries! I don't believe tin foil hats work for that.

We just have to accept that cooties happen, and they happen because clients drop their dramas and traumas at our feet. Their crises carry intense emotions and have enormous amounts of energy attached to them, which is usually negative energy. The more intense the emotions and energies are, the more you can be affected. So, boundaries, boundaries, boundaries!

Let me be clear about this. Maintaining personal boundaries doesn't mean that you don't care about your clients. What it does mean is that you don't take on their "stuff." It means that when your client leaves you—whether they walk out of your office, or you hang up the phone, or you shut down the computer—you go on with your normal life unaffected by what you dealt with. Essentially, you can go off and have a happy day. It also means you can sleep soundly and that a client's woes aren't keeping you awake—and, most of all, you're not dreaming about them. If you're dreaming about them, your energetic boundaries have surely been breached.

Hand-in-hand with setting boundaries is the ability and willingness to say one of the most difficult one-syllable words ever: NO. For a great many spiritual people saying "no" and meaning it, isn't such an easy thing to do. But mastering the use of the word "no" and using it as often as necessary, will contribute greatly to your well-being. So, say it here and now: NO. Again: NO. Say it louder: **NO**. Say it like you mean it: **NO! NO! NO!** That feels pretty good, no?!

Becoming comfortable and fluent with "no" will serve you well when clients try to push your limits—assuming you've set limits, a.k.a., boundaries. And, believe me, your limits will be tested! Most of your clients will be respectful and considerate of your time, but you can bet that there'll be those few.

One of the ways in which *those few* will try to push the limits is in their access to you—as in that they believe that they should always have access to you and that you're supposed to be available to them at any given moment. A word to the wise here: deny access and hold your boundaries! Don't feel obligated to be "on call" every hour of every day! To say the least, being available 24/7 is not in the best interest of your well-being.

Although you needn't be at everyone's beck and call, work with your clients in scheduling their appointments. Be as flexible and as accommodating as you can be without sacrificing your own well-being. Many, if not most, of your appointments might have to be scheduled for after normal working hours or on the weekends. A "check-up" with one's psychic is, unfortunately, still not considered an excusable absence from work!

Also, be prepared for the calls of crises. Clients will call when they're in crisis. And, we know, crises know no time, but be discerning. Your client may *feel* that their situation is a crisis. Good grief, we've all been there. When we're in the midst of a distressing situation, it can make us a wee bit less than objective about what's really urgent, making the situation feel like a crisis! Consequently, before you drop everything you're doing, determine whether or not it's a legitimate crisis; moreover, that it's a crisis that you can help with. Frankly, and not to diminish how helpful a psychic reading can be, if it *is* a major crisis, your client will probably be helped more by seeing another kind of professional, i.e., their therapist, a chiropractor, an attorney, their shaman, their acupuncturist, or an exorcist. Or, they might need to call 911. If any of those would be more appropriate, don't hesitate to advise them to get that help.

If you deem their situation doesn't require an exorcist, but is serious, keep in mind that you're still not obligated to drop everything you're doing. It's okay to say, *"No, I can't do a reading for you today* (or whatever day/time they're dictating to you), *but I have these other days and times open and I would be very happy to meet with you then."* Accommodate your clientele, but you are absolutely, positively not required to be available at their summoning. That is not good for your well-being.

Set your limits and screen your calls! Have you ever had the experience where you blindly answered a call and it was a client on the other end that took your "hello" as their green light to erupt about their unfolding drama? And then they expected you to do a reading for them on the spot! Most of us, unfortunately, know that kind of call all too well. And for most of us, just one of those is enough to let all "unknown" calls go to voicemail. Thanks to the great Gods of Technology, we can easily avoid those shock waves of energy. Nowadays, we have the luxury of using voicemail, email, text, Facebook, and other digital media, to listen to or read our messages, and then get back to our clients at our convenience. Of even more significance, we can get back to them when we're braced for them. But if you dare to answer your phone before looking at caller id and the floodgates open, remember to use the all-powerful "NO" to stop the deluge!

Mastering the usage of "NO" will also help in sustaining a life outside of being a psychic. Just a little bit of soft advice: NEVER GIVE UP YOUR PERSONAL LIFE! There's no way to have well-being without having a personal life. There's a saying that goes, "All work and no play makes for some really out-of-whack psychics" .....or something like that anyway. You've got to create the time for yourself, your family, your friends, your pets, and then some more time for yourself. I emphasize that because those of us who are in service tend to forget the "self" part!

One of the best ways I can suggest to create the time for YOU is to get a marker, look at your calendar a week, or a month, in advance, and mark off blocks of time. If your mate's day off from work is Thursday, mark out Thursdays. If your bungee-jumping group hangs together every second Saturday of the month, cross those Saturdays off. Make sure to get your children's activities marked on your calendar as soon as you're informed of them. Now, last, but absolutely not least, block out the time for you solo. If you meditate for twenty minutes a day and you need a reminder, block out those twenty minutes. Perhaps you have a couple of favorite programs you enjoy watching, then earmark the times that they're on. Or, maybe you just "don't do Mondays." In that case, don't! Block out all of your Mondays with your initials big and bold!! After you've allocated the time for those important things in life, then go ahead and fill up your calendar with appointments.

Before you start filling up your calendar from morning until night with appointments, though, I'd recommend that you give some thought to what times of the day you're at your best. Are you aware of what your optimum times to work are? Some of us don't pay much attention to how our daily energy cycles ebb and flow, but we should if we want to be healthier, happier people—and better psychics. When we're aware of when our energy peaks and when it dips, we can work with our cycle and not against it. Working against it is like when we're on the down-slide and we just grab some more caffeine, carbs, or sugar, and plod through. You'd be doing your well-being a great big favor by getting to know your body clock and your biorhythms, and then, if possible, schedule your appointments accordingly. Now, don't get me wrong, I'm not saying that we're disconnected from Spirit or can't be intuitive when we're in a dip. That's not it at all. What I mean is that we're just not running on all cylinders, and thus, it takes more effort to have the wherewithal do a reading—and doing readings takes wherewithal.

For instance, I'm not an early morning intuitive, and that's a colossal understatement that my Guides will attest to! I'm generally up and moving around early enough. I'll walk my dogs, I'll go for a run, I'll talk to my chickens, but I don't talk much to my husband because *he says* I don't make a lot of sense. My hotline to other dimensions, however, is still on snooze!! I know that it's best for me to ease into my day. Therefore, as a rule, I don't schedule any appointments before noon. My clients are okay with that, as they should be, because it's in their best interest, after all, that I'm functioning at my optimum—and that I'm intelligible.

Rest assured that your clientele will be okay with how you work, too. Maybe you're an A.M. adviser, and, if so, then try to schedule your sessions early in the day. Or, perhaps you function better in the P.M. In that case, book your appointments late in the day or evenings. Then again, maybe you're one of the lucky ones who can communicate with non-physical, as well as with physical beings (which are the hardest) any time of the day or night. My hat is off to you! But if you're like most of us, there are certain times when it just takes more effort to get into gear—or the gears are completely jammed! So, don't force it if you don't have to. Ascertain when you're at your best, which will guarantee that you'll be doing your best, for your clients, for your practice, and best of all, for your own well-being.

Now, belaboring what probably seems like the never-ending topic of boundaries. I said at the beginning of this chapter that this is one of the most important chapters of all, and discussing the alpha to omega of boundaries is primarily why. It can't be stressed enough that when you do this work and you don't establish and keep strong boundaries you won't have well-being. So, belabor on I must.

Most of us who are in the service fields are kindhearted people whose kindness knows no bounds. That may sound like an admirable quality, but it's not; it's actually unhealthy. Having no bounds means you leave yourself wide open to take on what's not yours, emotionally, energetically, even physically. So, heed this advice: get some bounds and don't be afraid to use them!

One way you use them is when you hold firm in your knowing that your clients' troubles are theirs and theirs alone. The saying goes, "Misery loves company," and people in crisis will try to draw you into their crisis. For your own well-being, don't go there. Always keep in the forefront of your mind that your only role is to be a voice for Infinite Intelligence. As I mentioned earlier, help them in ways that you can, such as suggesting books, CDs, therapy, hypnosis, or even rehab. Just remember, all you can do is make suggestions. It's that *"You can lead a horse to water but can't make them drink it"* thing. Which means that, after you've imparted their messages to them and offered guidance they could benefit from, send them on their way. That's not being cold or calloused. It's karmically correct that you don't assume their learning experience. Seriously, do any of us *really* need to add to our own repertoire of learning experiences?! And, by the way, whatever you do, avoid the temptation to tell a client to call you *any time*—BECAUSE THEY WILL! In the early days of my practice I made that mistake. It was yet another rude awakening for me. I mean literally a rude awakening, as in being awakened at 2 a.m.!

Maintaining your well-being requires that you, in no way, take on your clients' karma, their life lessons, or plant yourself into the reality they're creating for themselves. I'll also point out that not one among us is The Savior sent from above to save all mankind! For Christ's sake, remember what happened to the last guy who took that on?! Besides, stigmata is hell on gloves.

It's also important to hold your boundaries so that clients can't take from you. They're known as energy drainers. You can count on having the occasional client come to you who will deplete your energy, unbeknownst to them and, unfortunately, you. But the sooner it can be *beknownst* to you, the better off you'll fare. We all know those types of people. They're the kind you run into at the grocery store who will talk and talk and talk and talk, and then talk some more. Then they say, "Gotta go, goodbye." You stand there thinking, "Oh my God, I think I need a nap!" In a session with you, these people will talk and talk and talk and talk, and talk some more, and then ask you, "So what do you think?" In your foggy state you'll try to tune in and your Guides will say, "Huh, what's going on? What did you want to know? We were taking a nap." The sooner you can recognize what's going on, the sooner you can and should shield your energy field and take control of the reading.

But wait, there's more, and it's a lot more damaging. And those are the all-out psychic vampires. These individuals absolutely KNOW that they're draining your energy because that's what they're intending to do. Deliberately. (A lot of these people dabble with the Dark Side, so, literally, the Devil may have made them do it.) Regrettably, we don't always recognize them quickly enough because they look normal enough. And we're not aware at the time that it's happening what they're up to since a lack of clarity is one of the symptoms. Staying tuned in to how you're feeling is your best line of defense. Otherwise, after they've gone, that individual will leave the session feeling invigorated and revitalized. You, on the other hand, will have had your life force energy sucked out of you— and that is not an exaggeration. To be blunt, you'll feel like crap. And you'll definitely need of a nap.

When the vampire calls for another appointment, and you can bet they will—after all, they're thinking, *yum, fresh energy!*—you can, of course, fortify your energetic boundaries so that you can't be drained. But why subject yourself to that? It would be better to take the opportunity to use that powerful word: "NO!" It's your business, therefore, it's your prerogative to work with those whom you choose to—and not work with those you choose not to work with. Besides, it's your well-being on the line. Tell the vampire to go suck somewhere else.

Sometimes, though, we don't have the luxury of picking and choosing the people we read for. That's the case if you work psychic faires, private parties, festivals, and other big events. In any of those arenas you'll have a different person sitting in front of you every fifteen, twenty, or thirty minutes. Prepare for it!

These events can be exciting to participate in, they can be very profitable, and they can be a great way to expand clientele. Yay for all of the above! But working big events can be intensely taxing on all levels of your being. That stands to reason because not only are we interacting with client after client, but we're doing so while being psychically wide-open, all the while being immersed in a supersaturated sea of energies. If that wasn't enough, we're trying to keep the integrity of our own energy field at the same time. Phew, that's taxing just to think about! And so, the boy scout motto applies: be prepared.

The preparation starts by getting a couple of nights of good sleep before the event. Since most faires are held on Saturdays and/or Sundays, you might consider skipping Friday night's happy hour with the gang. A hungover psychic is ill-prepared for a parade of clients or for those environments—and can potentially smell bad to boot. Do yourself a favor and get rested up. Party after the event.

When you get to the venue, prepare yourself and your designated space with whatever means or manner works for you. We all have our own inimitable style. Whether you surround yourself with white light, envision mirrors facing outward from you, use a grid of crystals or stones, etc., it doesn't matter. What matters is that you clear your space and establish your boundaries.

During the event, be sure to stay hydrated and take breaks as often as needed to stay grounded and clear. Find out ahead of time if food will be available. If not, bring your lunch, and then be sure that you make yourself stop to eat it! Pack easy to nosh snacks (preferably non-sticky to the hands) to nibble on between clients. Doing so will help to keep your energy up—and you'll avoid having to speak louder because your stomach is growling!

And, for your utmost comfort and well-being, whatever you do, don't wait until your eyeballs are floating before you take a bathroom break!

Post-event, if at all feasible for you, take the next day off or, at the very least, limit your schedule. But the encouragement is to take the day off. If you had a good faire, and particularly if it was an entire weekend, you WILL be spent in more ways than you may even realize. That's especially true for the first few faires or big events you participate in. When I first began working big faires I would feel like I had the flu the day after. It only took a couple of times of feeling bad for me to realize that I needed to allow myself a day of recuperation. My suggestion to you is to allow yourself the time you need to recuperate. Truly, it will save you the hassle of canceling appointments or calling in sick to a job. After a while, though, and the more you work these kinds of events, you'll find that the amount of time you need to recover will become less and less. It's just like any exercise, the more you do it the stronger you become and the greater your capacity becomes. Consequently, the more you exercise your psychic muscles, the stronger those muscles get and the more psychic weight you can handle for longer periods of time. And just the same as it is in physical exercise, time off and rest are necessities, not luxuries.

Even if you haven't worked an extravaganza, just the nature of this work alone WILL drain you. If you have a pretty good-sized practice, the draining is cumulative, so you WILL need to take time off routinely to replenish. Just for the record, the fact that we get drained is nothing to be ashamed of. As a matter of fact, I'd go so far as to say that if you're not totally wiped out from time-to-time, you're either not working a lot yet or you're not giving it your all.

When we get depleted, we've got to fill ourselves back up. I'll remind you here, as I often have to remind myself, that you have to *make* the time, not *try* to *find* the time—because we never find the time. When it comes to ourselves and, particularly our time, when we say we're going to "try," we usually don't try hard enough. When we say "find," we typically don't find it, because we didn't really try. Which means that we allow our time to be taken up by someone or something else we deem more important than ourselves. So then, you have to **make** the time. What you'll also be making is an investment in your well-being that will yield healthy returns.

As I said earlier in this chapter, the ideal way to plan for YOU time is by literally blocking out your calendar with permanent marker, or a big, bold font on your computer or phone. Then, allow yourself the pleasure of the 3-Rs: Release, Recharge, and Revive.

Release:

What has to be released is any and all energies that might have accumulated in your auric field or have become attached to you. Even when we're super careful and have strong boundaries, we don't always walk away from our sessions—or from Wal-Mart—clear or alone. Occasionally, we'll pick up cooties (especially in Wal-Mart!). And, every once in a while, you'll have a client's dead relative take a liking to you, and Great Grandpa may decide that he wants to hang out with you for a while. He may be a harmless non-physical fellow, nevertheless, he needs to go—unless, of course, he picks winning lottery numbers for you!

What also has to be released and processed is what gets stirred up emotionally for you. Let's be honest, unless you're a pathological narcissist or a humanoid robot, you're gonna have issues, and they're gonna get triggered. There's no way that you couldn't get triggered when you have clients parading in and out and their readings are about things that hit close to home. It's those damned voicemails from The Universe!! Don't wait until your mailbox is full, release the energy of the issue(s).

The main thing is, take breaks, and take breaks often.

Recharge:

This is a challenge for ALOT of people, although it's something that we should take delight in and savor as the treat that it is. What makes it a challenge then? Well, in the first place, it's because so many of us don't recognize that our battery is low—or completely drained—and needs recharging. I actually think that most of us do a better job of monitoring when our vehicle needs refueling and when our gadgets need to be charged, i.e., computers, phones, etc., than we do at realizing our own need for refueling and recharging. Too often it takes getting sick before the realization hits. Another thing is that it seems to be a challenge for some of us to grant ourselves permission to allow the time to fill back up after being depleted. Suggestion: give yourself permission.

Recharging means different things to different people. Also, what it takes to recharge will be vary depending on what you've dealt with and on how depleted you are. Sometimes it'll be enough to eat a good meal, to take a hot bath, to get a massage, or to just get lost in mindless television for an evening. Other times, like if you've been psychic marathoning, you'll need a full-fledged vacation! The following are a few surefire ways to recharge the mind, body, and spirit:

Eat:

The first and most obvious place to begin replenishment is with your physical apparatus. Basically, your body needs to be fed for optimum performance and well-being, and unless you were raised by a pack of wild boars, you know that you should eat healthy to be healthy, and blah, blah, blah, blah, blah. Yeah, I hear that, that's why I'm not getting up on a soapbox now to pontificate about healthy eating. Instead, I'll make you privy to some great forbidden knowledge about what to feed your body when it's depleted. Ready for it? Here it is: You feed it whatever it wants. You're feeling all the wiser now, aren't ya?!

Our bodies' intelligence knows what it needs at any given moment, and it tells us loud and clear by the cravings we get. Just as it is with any other workout, after a psychic workout it's natural to crave certain foods. The longer or more intense the psychic workout, the stronger the cravings, particularly for protein, trace minerals, and fat. Psychic work takes energy, burns calories, and minerals get leached from the body, so don't be surprised that you find yourself desiring foods that you don't typically eat. Maybe under normal circumstances you're a carb-aholic, but when you've been taxed you may feel like you have to have protein, or some fatty food, or chocolate—or chocolate *with* everything else! Overall, expect to experience powerful cravings for virtually anything considered a "comfort" food (chips and salsa for me......followed by ice cream!). At those times, the best thing to do is to give your body what it's asking for. When you need grounding and your energy reservoir is low, food is your friend and ally. These are not the times to be overly rigid about your diet. Allow yourself to indulge a bit.

Let's be clear here, though, I'm talking about indulging when we're depleted, like coming off a two-day psychic faire, or reading for twelve people back-to-back, or reading for your relatives—that'll take it out of you! I'm not suggesting eating a large pizza with all the toppings because you did one hour-long reading—even if it was for a relative!

Meditation:

In some form or another, meditation is probably THE most efficient and effective means for healing and recharging the mind, body, and spirit. Blocking out a little time on a daily basis to be in a state of *just being* calms the mind, and therefore the emotions, which then helps to restore the physical body from the cellular level outward. Although meditation has become a more accepted therapy in the mainstream, it's still not universally understood. There still are misconceptions about what meditation is and how it works. Don't take my word for it, see for yourself by asking a few of your clients what they think about meditation. Some, for sure, might actually practice it regularly. But don't be surprised by what others might tell you. Like those who believe that meditating means you have to sit in a fog of incense with your body twisted up like a pretzel all the while chanting or *OOOOOMMMMM*-ing for hours and hours. For crying out loud, no wonder it's not a common practice! First of all, it sounds freaky!! And just being practical, who has the time—or the flexibility—for that??!!

I have to wonder, though, if some of us psychics don't believe that same thing. I mean, why else wouldn't we all be sure to incorporate meditation into our lives and actually do it every day? I have to admit that I'm guilty as charged. We tend not to make the time because we have our lives, which includes family obligations, jobs, social events, television shows, and, of course, books to read on how to meditate.

In a perfect world, we would all have thirty or sixty minutes a day to set aside to sit in our sacred space to completely quiet our minds and bask in utter stillness. But, *hello*, this is the real world! Yet, even in our real world, most of us can certainly take a fifteen-minute time-out to regroup and restore some equilibrium in our lives. As far as a sacred space goes, hell, sometimes we just have to settle for the room with the porcelain seat! Really. It probably already has a scented candle, giving you some aromatherapy and bit of ambiance. All you'll need to do is to put out a "do not disturb" sign, lock the door, take a seat on the throne, and enjoy your fifteen minutes!

That's for a conventional meditation, but that's not the only option we have. Thankfully, meditation isn't "one size fits all." I compare it to exercise. It's a fact that thirty minutes of daily exercise is good for us, but it's also been proven that if we do the same exercise day after day, the benefits diminish because the body acclimates to it—besides, it gets *b-o-r-i-n-g*. The good news is that health experts say that those recommended thirty minutes don't have to be done all at once to be beneficial and that they can be done incrementally throughout the day. I believe that's also true with meditation. It doesn't have to be the same meditation day after day, and it doesn't have to be done all at one time. So, for those of us who need options and variety, here are a few suggestions for meditation, without formally calling them "meditations." These are convenient and practical ways to medita.....I mean.....to quiet the mind. Two, three, or however many of these moments, can easily be folded into a daily routine:

* Whatever you do first thing in the morning, don't jump out of bed, unless you *really* have to pee or you're *really really* late for work! Instead, take at least five minutes, more if you have that luxury, to smoothly transition from your sleep state into waking. Say "good morning" to God, your angels, the world, the new day, your Self. Stretch your body and appreciate it. Set your intention to have a wonderful day. Taking these first few moments in the a.m. to get centered can literally make or break your entire day. If you have a family that relies on you to help get them out the door in the mornings, consider rising a few minutes earlier than everyone else. When you begin your days centered, you're less likely to get rattled or thrown off by anyone else's chaos. Don't underestimate the power of your centeredness to influence everyone else in your household—two-legged and four-legged alike!

Talking about the power of influence, let me suggest that you think twice about turning on the television first thing for the morning news. That's the antithesis of quieting the mind. Do you really want to start out your day in the vibration of death, doom, and destruction?! Even if the morning crew wraps up the broadcast with, *"Have a great day everyone!"* Right......

* Sit and savor your morning cup of coffee, tea, mimosa, or whatever tickles your palate, for at least fifteen or twenty minutes. Sit by a window or outside on a porch or balcony (if you have one and if weather permits). Appreciate whatever nature you have in your environment: birds, wildlife, plants, trees, weird neighbors.

* Take a mid-day break. If you work a job that's indoors, get outside at breaktime or lunch. Take a little walk, sit in your car, detach from the energy of the work environment, and soak up some Vitamin D. The same advice holds true even if you work from home: take a little walk, detach from the energy of whatever you're doing at home, soak up some Vitamin D. Many of us forget to take a break and get outside for a bit when we're at home. That's a big mistake. Set an alarm and GET OUT!!!!

* Wrap up the day by relaxing in your favorite chair for twenty or thirty minutes. Sit in the backyard, on a balcony, in your living room, or yes, in the bathroom if that's where you need to go. Sip a glass of wine, drink a cup of herbal tea, relish a piece of fruit, indulge in a bit of chocolate. Consciously sweep away the day.

* End the day with a long, hot, tranquil soak in a bathtub. Scented or not, with bubbles or without, rubber ducky or alone, it's your call. Lounging in water will clear the mind and relax the body from the rat-a-tat of a hectic day.

* Anytime of the day or night, from wherever you are, take a moment to focus on the fabulous gifts we're given by Ms. Mother Nature, namely, the seasons. Each one has its own uniquely beautiful and mind-quieting—and mind-blowing— gifts to offer. Let yourself be awed and renewed by the

rebirth that is spring, sync up and slow down with the pace of summer, appreciate the harvest of autumn in all its colorful glory. In winter, shift your focus from griping about the cold or a snow storm and turn it into a meditation of gratefulness for the whitewashing and the stillness that is blanketing your little part of the world, as well as for winter's message: take time to hibernate, to rest, to prepare yourself for the next new cycle.

* Appreciate what you see in, and what falls from, Sir Father Sky. By day, be a spectator and interpreter of the cloud pictures moving overhead. Watch raindrops or snowflakes fall. Then let the magic of the night sky amaze you. Compliments of the Universe, there's not a more magnificent canvas to marvel at and get lost in. Look up to the heavens, count stars or just watch them twinkle. Let your mind wander among the celestial bodies. Stare at the moon (howl if you wish, just make sure that your neighbors won't call the cops) and soak up the moon beams. Be dazzled by a lightning show—from a safe distance, of course! Or watch for UFOs!!

* Take a walking meditation. Slow or fast, with your dogs or without, outside or inside, on a treadmill, with music or sans music. You decide, it's your meditative walk. For the sake of clearing your mind, however, it might be best to walk without another human. You know how "they" like to talk, and that would negate the meditation part. Unless, of course, you're both in agreement about the right to remain silent.

* Do some other form of a moving meditation, such as yoga, tai chi, chi gong, hiking, etc. Even rock-climbing. It takes a tremendous amount of concentration to ascend and descend safely. Safety is paramount in rock-climbing so there's absolutely no place in the mind for chatter!

* Another on the run meditation is, literally, running or jogging. This is actually my meditation of choice. Strange as it sounds, it's running with headphones playing loud music, mostly to drown out my huffing and puffing so I don't think

I'm dying. For those of us who like to run, there's truly nothing else that clears and calms the mind and gets us out of our overactive gray matter!

As I said, those suggestions are just a few ways to grab a bit of quietude here and there. Even if your life isn't known for its quietude!

Perhaps, though, that you're someone who prefers a more formal or structured meditation. If you're a solitary meditator, but want a guided meditation, there are plenty of really great CDs and DVDs available. Should your preference be meditating in community, find a local group that meets once or twice a week. Or, if you're so inclined, start your own meditation group!

The whatever, however, whenever, you make the time for stillness doesn't matter. What matters is that you do your darnedest not to let it get to the "hardly ever" point. Find your own way to get out of your chattering monkey brain, and then just do it. If you're not sure about what resonates best with you, my suggestion would that you meditate on it!

Virtual Escapes:

It's a scary thing being in our own heads 24/7 with all our "stuff" swirling around up there. Making it even worse is that sometimes, even with incredibly sturdy boundaries, we'll also have client "files" adding to the swirl. Our well-being doesn't stand a chance with all that swirling going on! In order to recharge then, we need to virtually escape, to take a psychic holiday. Basically, we need to be out of our minds!

Here's just a sampling of some ways to virtual escape:

Books:

Give yourself permission to read books other than those that are metaphysically-oriented. In other words, take a break from perpetual studying, occulting, self-helping, or New Aging! Every once in a while, pick up a trashy novel, a laughably predictable whodunit, a book of stupid sophomoric jokes. Read poetry, or biographies of people you admire, or whatever other genre floats your boat. Allow your mind to explore and escape to other places and times.

Movies:

Watch films that make you laugh, make you cry, and then make you laugh and cry some more. Getting absorbed in a movie is a great way to release tension and pent up emotions (although maybe not a thriller). Sit in a theater, pop in a DVD, or call up one of the movies you've recorded that you said you'd watch some day. Sit back and forget everything and everybody for a brief time. Allow yourself to be transported elsewhere. Or, just enjoy the luxury of being entertained.

Body Work:

Get a massage. Have acupuncture or acupressure done. Get a manicure or pedicure. Have some energy work done. Give yourself the gift of a healer's gift.

Gardening:

Plant, prune, pull weeds, walk around with a hose watering flowers, vegetables, herbs, or trees. Talk to the foliage (make sure the neighbors aren't watching!). Get your hands dirty. Ground yourself in rich earth energy.

Crafts and Hobbies:

Become absorbed in creating. Whether you enjoy knitting, pottery, painting, floral-design, stamp-collecting, crossword puzzles, writing, model building, woodworking, jewelry-making, etc., etc., etc. Get completely lost in a creative project.

Classes:

Sign up to take a class. We all have something that we've always wanted to learn about or have wanted to learn how to do. We say we'll do it someday. Why not make someday now? Check out what's being offered by your local community college or specialty stores, i.e., rock shops for lapidary, book stores for writing, herb stores for remedies, yoga studios for, well, obviously, for yoga, etc. Learn something new. Expand your mind.

Music:
The listening to or the making of. Different types of music can take us psychically, mentally, and emotionally to different places. Transcend your being with New Age music, Native American drumming, or Buddhist chanting. Go down memory lane with oldies—some of our lanes are longer and older than others, so we have a lot to choose from—or play air guitar to rock or heavy metal. If you play an instrument, make your own music. It might be a didgeridoo you become one with, a drum set that you beat your stress out on, or strum a guitar to something folksy.

Dance:
Get off your butt, get your groove on, get down and shake your bootie! Dance around the house to rock & roll, gyrate your body to the rhythms of salsa, or hip and hop to hip-hop! Belly-dance, pirouette and leap, or trance-dance into other realms. Grab a partner and dosy-doe or do the tango. Dance to feel your body being alive. Move your body to let your Soul dance.

Children:
Play with your children or grandchildren if you have them. Don't play just to entertain them or to wear their little limitless-energy selves out or because you feel you have to. Play with children because you want to. Play with them because playing is a fun thing. Let them teach you how to play and have fun.

Dogs, Cats, and Other Pets:
Dogs are unconditional love and pure, unbridled joy. They're always up for whatever you need, whether it's sitting, walking, or taking naps. From our dogs, we can learn how to be in the present moment, in the now. Your dogs can be the greatest meditation buddies ever!

If you're a cat person, watch how curious your feline is about the world around them—or anything that dangles—and let it spark your own curiosity about the world! Cuddle with your cat and allow yourself to be lulled by its purring. Sit and pet your cat and observe how it soothes your mind and body.

Ride a horse, talk to a horse, love a horse—it's the best therapy whether it's bareback, saddled, or just communing.

Raise chickens as pets. I LOVE MY CHICKIES! I never could have, would have, imagined myself saying that—until I got them!! They are smart, sweet, funny, and affectionate. Chickens will make one become more mindful. Mostly it's being mindful about where one steps......they shit a lot and shit everywhere.

Hamsters, ferrets, pigs, turtles, canaries, parakeets, fish, it doesn't matter what kind of critter you bond with and exchange love energy with. What matters is that it gives you pause—or paws—and makes you smile from the inside out.

Nature:

Get outside in nature. No matter what kind of area you live in, find some nature. Even in a very urban area there's nature to be found. Find a park or frequent your city's botanical gardens. No matter what season it is, get outside. There is nothing more healing, balancing, or restorative than nature. Revel in the abundance of nature. Soak up rays of the sun or some negative ions. Soak up Source. Getting out in nature guarantees well-being.

Healing Places:

Do you have a special place that you consider healing, mystical, or magical? It can be a church, chapel, or a temple, but it doesn't have to be. Perhaps it's a rock you like to sit on off your favorite hiking trail, or a secluded spot of a nearby beach, or the roof of your apartment building. Or else, it can be your favorite museum in which you wander around and lose track of time or a nearby park which has a pond, a fountain, or a little gazebo to sit in. Even still, maybe you have a great backyard that gives you the solace you need. It's not important where or what it is for you, it's important how you feel being there. The thing is, it doesn't have to be a special location, it just has to be special to you. Find your place of healing and quietude and then escape to it often.

Technology—Not:

Disconnect yourself. Turn off your cellphone and don't turn on your computer. Yes, they *do* have off buttons! Yes, you *will* suffer withdrawal. Try doing it for a day. Okay, for half a day. Alright, maybe for just three or four hours. How about just two hours? At least an hour......

Friends:

By far, THE most important component of one's well-being is having friends—and that's a scientifically-proven fact. Google it! Having a few good friends to rely on, to lean on, to have fun and laugh with is critical to our well-being. Make time OFTEN to get together with friends to relax, to enjoy your connection to them, and to recharge your being. Friends are even better than having chickens!

Vacation:

Take a vacation. Get out of town. Or, at the very least, close down shop and just tell people you're out of town—then act as if you are! Take a vacation. Of course, that means you might also have to turn off your cellphone......I'm just sayin'. Take a vacation. Go somewhere you've never been or else return to someplace you love. Take a vacation. A change of scenery, a break from the daily grind, time for leisure and pleasure and play. The point I'm trying to make is that you gotta take a vacation!

If for some reason you can't go away somewhere or don't want to, at least take some time off from your everyday life and do some "vacationy" things: sight-see around your own town, lay out in the sun, hang out at the house and read your stash of trashy novels, or catch up on your soap operas! Most of all, refrain from checking your texts every fifteen minutes and let your calls go to voicemail—remember, you're on vacation!

I'm sure you agree that these suggestions sound really good. After all, who doesn't want to be able to do a meditation, lounge and read a book, take a long bath, or just do whatever it is that they want to do? Yet, I hear the *yeah, yeah, yeah, BUT*—but I have a job, but I have a mate, but I have kids, but I have humanity to serve. The biggest "but" I hear is, ***but*** *you don't understand, lady, because you must live in fantasyland and don't have a clue of what* real *life is!* Well, I'll tell you, I do know about real life. As a matter of fact, I actually have one, and that's how I know so well of what I speak. I especially know first-hand what happens when we don't forge out a bit of time for ourselves on a regular basis. It's not pretty what happens. So, from that first-hand experience, I strongly encourage you to schedule downtime for yourself—and don't wait for circumstances to dictate that you *have* to.

<u>Revive:</u>

When you make it a priority to release what's not yours, when you clear your energy field, and when you allow yourself to fully recharge, reviving is what your Self—body, mind, and spirit—will just naturally do, and then you'll have experienced more reviving than a bunch of Southern Baptists under an excruciatingly hot tent in the middle of July!

*

In the business of being psychic, your well-being goes hand-in-hand with your psychicness. You won't have one without the other. We have to be up for this work physically, mentally, emotionally, and psychically. But we also have to know when to put down the work from time to time. All psychic, all the time, is not conducive to one's well-being. But, heck, you knew that— you're psychic!

CHAPTER 10:

YOUR SUPPORT SYSTEM

Source always has our back, and good God (which God is), we couldn't ask for a better support system. Actually, Source is the only support we ever really need. Unfortunately, though, we don't always remember that. When we're stuck in our stuff we tend to feel alone, maybe even forgotten. When we're in our humanness we want tangible, proof-positive help that we can see, hear, feel, and see some more. Basically, our in-body selves need to have support systems on this plane of existence in the form of other in-bodies, and because we're that way, it's important for us to develop those support systems.

We humans need our communities. We need our packs. We need our tribes. We need our other "birds-of-a-feather." Regardless of the label we give them, these are our support systems. These are the people who lend support to us when we need it and we, in turn, lend our support to them when they're in need. We help each other to stay grounded and balanced, and help each other up when we're down. And, the *piece de resistance* is that these are the people we get together with to play, laugh, and have fun. For all of these reasons and more, people need people.

For psychics, finding a good support system sometimes takes a little more effort. To say that Lightworkers march to the beat of a different drummer is a ridiculously big fat understatement! It's a waaaay different drummer with a waaaay different beat!! Given that, the challenge for us is finding our communities, tribes, packs, flocks, etc., who share our paradiddles, or who will support us even if they don't—or don't want to—understand the different drumming. What's more, there are "layers" to our support systems, with the first layer being the most up close and personal to us, and then extending out from there.

The first and most significant layer is made up of those nearest and dearest to us, which would be the people we live with. If you're blessed to live with people who are supportive of you, you should give thanks for them every single day of your life for the treasures that they are. Even if they don't completely "get" you, or don't understand exactly what it is that you do, it's an advantage to have their unconditional acceptance. Let me assure you, not all psychics are so blessed with such treasures. Living with people that support you will make doing this work so much easier. For that matter, it will make life for you better overall.

Our home should be our sanctuary and, ideally, we should be able to find sanctuary with those we live with. In a perfect world, our family dynamics would be peaceful, harmonious, joyful, and straight of out of a 1950's television show! But, alas, this isn't a perfect world. If you live alone, of course you're much better able to create that ideal environment for yourself, you lucky dog! On the other hand, if you're like most of us, you share your home with a partner, with children, or with housemates—which means good luck with creating that utopia or Beaver Cleaver world! Let's be honest, in and of itself, cohabitation is difficult enough, but the whole "psychic thing" adds another entirely different kind of ingredient to the mixture. If those you live with have issues with "that weird thing you do," home life could be, let's just say, a bit challenging. And a challenging home life is anything but a sanctuary. Needless to say, that's not the definition of a support system.

Before addressing any challenge that might be present in your home life, let's look at it from the eyes of the opposition. In all fairness to them, choosing to make your money as a fortune-teller, which are their words, not mine (I know this because they've been used on me) isn't what could be called a conventional, run-of-the-mill, or esteemed career choice. From that perspective, it's not unreasonable that you might meet with some disapproval, or even wariness. If this is a situation you face, I'd suggest that rather than get defensive or combative—and have your house divided—try to put yourself in their shoes, albeit momentarily ('cause them is some pretty narrow shoes!). Besides the fact that they need a good polishing, from those shoes you'll see that any disapproval comes from their lack of understanding, their ingrained beliefs, and the big one, fear. To say the least, they're definitely not hearing your drummer; at worst, they believe your drummer is Satan!

Understanding begets understanding. If you want your significant people to understand what it is that you actually do, as opposed to their beliefs about what you do, you've first got to understand them. Try to understand what frame of reference their opposition is coming from. Someone's religious beliefs, their personal dogma, or the opinions that they inherited from their upbringing, will cloud their perception of what your wicked ass (again, their words) is involved with. So, first and foremost, have patience with them and know that whatever it is that they've been indoctrinated with isn't going to be un-indoctrinated overnight. They'll need to be educated about the metaphysical world, and it's incumbent upon you to do that educating. After all, that's another hat that we wear when we choose to do this work, the one of spiritual educator. And how do you educate them? The short answer is: by example.

As I said, the primary reason for someone's aversion to psychics and spiritualism is fear—besides reading *The National Enquirer* and watching televangelists! That fear comes from misinformation they've gotten along their way about psychics and readings and all other hocus-pocus, which makes for some very misguided beliefs. Probably the biggest fear—and most laughable to anyone who knows better—stems from the belief that if a person is psychic, they're certainly in cahoots with the Devil or the Dark Side. Or maybe it's zombies or vampires, because according to Hollywood the un-dead are the fashionable fears these days!

The task before you then is to try to allay their fears. How do you allay their fears, you ask? Well, I'll tell you how, but first let me suggest two things NOT to do: don't laugh at them and don't argue with them. I'll elaborate.

Although there are some outrageous notions that people have about the psychic world, some that are so unbelievably ridiculous that they make us laugh so hard we could just pee our pants—which, by the way, don't do, because they'll think the Devil made you lose control—but don't laugh. Seriously, be sensitive to anyone who's sharing their fears with you. Remember, you're putting yourself in their shoes, and from their shoes those fears are real and frightening. If you have to, pretend they're a client. As a professional psychic, you're gonna hear all kinds of far-out-there wonky-wacky crap! And as a professional, you wouldn't laugh at a client's wonky-wacky crap, right? Right. So, afford the significant people in your life the same courtesy. If all else fails, bite your lip until it bleeds. When you taste blood in your mouth you definitely won't feel like laughing. But don't let it drip or you'll reinforce the vampire suspicion.

Next, don't argue with them. No good and no convincing can come from arguing with someone about what you *don't* do. If you engage them in an argument, all that'll happen is that you'll wind up off the subject that matters. For example, let's say that your mate spies your deck of tarot cards on your desk. She or he believes it's the Devil's work and that you're on the straight path to Hell and by God, "by GOD!" they say, they're not going there with you! If you let your emotions get the best of you, you'll argue about the existence of the Devil, on what tarot cards are, on whether or not there's actually a Hell, on why on earth do you always leave the toilet seat like that (that *always* comes up in a household argument!). Note to self here: keep your cool and keep your eye on your goals. And the goals are to allay their fears, to achieve a tranquil home environment, to educate them, and, ultimately, to have them as a support system. So: Abort the argument! Abort the argument!!

The thing to do is to listen to them. Acknowledge their fears. Also, cut them some slack and recognize that a lot of their fears are *for you* because they care about you. Then, calmly and rationally, explain what it is that you do, all the while keeping in mind that any real success in allaying their fears will not be by what you say, but by what you do. Only in their observation of what you do and how you help people can their perception change. And have patience. Their fears will be put to rest when they see that you don't run off with a band of gypsies or perform rituals that sacrifice kittens. Of course, praying for Divine intervention helps, too.

Then again, sometimes we just have to agree to disagree with people. Try as you may to show them what a Lightworker is all about, your people may not be able to get beyond their own biases and dogmas. They are certainly entitled to their non-acceptance, which means that you've got to try to accept their non-acceptance. Hopefully there's enough love and respect between you that they'll continue to be supportive in the non-woo-woo areas of your life. Just don't talk shop at dinner time!

Sadly, not all family members are that generous. As a matter of fact, some home environments can become outright hostile territories. I've known many a budding psychic who had to hide their buds when they went home. If they didn't, they faced being belittled or taunted, or worse, given ultimatums about their living situation.

When I owned a metaphysical store, I "harbored" many closet practitioners of one kind or another: psychics, Wiccans, Buddhists, pagans, agnostics, you name it. The demographics of the area were predominantly conservative, patriarchal, Old World culture-steeped, Catholicism. It was certainly not a location I, myself, would've chosen for a New Age store. But I did what the voices told me to do.

This was a time before Meet-Up groups and other online arenas, so, in essence, my shop became a gathering place, or "safe-house" for us like-mindeds to be in community. On one hand, I was pleased that I could provide a safe place for them to be themselves; on the other hand, it made me sad that so many of these wonderful Light-filled, gifted beings were living double-lives. Their authentic selves would come in and purchase tarot cards, pendulums, runes, and various tools, and would be so excited about playing with their new "toys." Yet, they knew full well that at home the only playtime they might have would be when no one was around, when everyone else was asleep, or if they locked themselves in the bathroom.

So many purchases were made on the downlow that I felt like I was managing an adults-only novelty store and sending customers out with nondescript brown paper bags! It's true!! My customers would buy things that they couldn't openly carry into their own homes, such as books and ritual tools, even incense and candles. *Incense and candles, for crying out loud!* And, much, much, much, jewelry. Pentacles, ankhs, goddess charms, yin-yangs, yes, even alien heads that were destined to only be worn "under the cover of darkness," like under long sleeves, gloves, and high collars. Where these folks lived, if it wasn't a crucifix, rosary beads, or a WWJD piece of jewelry, it wasn't permissible.

This makes me wonder about the folks wearing the WWJD jewelry. Do they ever actually ask themselves the question, WHAT *WOULD* JESUS DO?! I bet Jesus would've used a lot of candles and incense because he'd think that their attitude stunk!!

But those were worse case scenarios. Hopefully you're not leading a double life or feel forced to be a closet psychic. I also hope that you're reading this book out in the open and not under the covers with a flashlight! Above all else, I hope you can count on those closest to you to be your biggest support system.

Even if you're graced to be living with people who are supportive of your practice, those same people may not support the idea of you practicing in the home you share with them. If your plan is to bring clients into the home, make sure that your cohabitants are comfortable with that plan. There may be any number of reasons why this isn't acceptable to them, but generally it tends to be a matter of privacy—or what they see as the loss of it. That's a valid reason. After all, there is indeed some privacy lost when you have various strangers traipsing in and out of your living space. The prospect of that can make anyone a bit uncomfortable, to say the least, and for anyone who's a private person by nature, a constant stream of people can feel extraordinarily invasive. The best thing you can do is call a family meeting, and if a housemate isn't comfortable with your clientele being in your home, respect their feelings—and their privacy. However, if everyone's on board, bring 'em on!

Before bringing your clientele into your home, however, there's something else to consider, and that's the particularly sensitive or empathic (besides yourself) members of the household who could be energetically impacted—especially your children and pets. Be ever mindful that your clients will always walk into your home with their emotional baggage. Besides that, they may not be walking into your home alone—dead Aunt Bertha may be tagging along! Heavy energy and dead relatives can and will affect those who are sensitive or those who don't know how to protect their energy fields. Even if you're diligent in clearing the energy, you may not be able to clear it out quick enough. If all of your housemates can maintain their own energetic integrity, there's nothing to be concerned about. But if they begin to sound a little like Aunt Bertha, well then, you may have a bit of a problem on your hands!

Never lose sight of the fact that a shared home should be a sanctuary for everyone who lives there. If you want your housemates to be a support system for you, you'll need to be supportive of them in return. So find the arrangement that works best for everyone.

Friendships are the next layer of your support system. True friends are pure gold. First, though, we'll look at when they're gold-plated, their gold rubs off, or when they're just gold-colored. In other words: fake.

When you begin or expand your professional practice, there may be some friends who, for various reasons, can't expand with you. Be prepared for that. For certain, a friend or two will be convinced that you've lost your mind! Then, there might be some friends who have very different beliefs and won't be able to accept the "whole psychic thing." What happens most often, though, is that some old friends simply won't be able to let go of the past. They just won't be able to let go of the person they knew you to be, whether that was who you were in high school, in college, or as their drinking buddy or party pal. In their retrospective eyes, you are the same old you, whomever that was. Frankly, these same people probably aren't evolving much themselves. You can recognize them by their big '80's hair or their mullets.

Old acquaintances aren't always considered friends, so it's not like you'd lose any real support, but don't be surprised if you become "un-friended" by a few of them on Facebook. It would likely be someone who knew you way-back-when who will hear or see online that you've become a psychic. They'll say something like, "A psychic?! No f*%#ing way!! Oh, dude, I gotta un-friend this freak!!!" If they're really religious, they probably won't say that. Instead, they'll say, "Oh dear Lord, I'll have to pray for her/him! But first I have to un-friend her/him."

We really do have to cut these people some slack on this, however. Let's face it, all of us have people in our memory banks that will forever be frozen as *that* person, the character they were back in the day. Think about people you knew ten, fifteen, twenty, or more years ago. Perhaps you had a buddy you partied *very hard* with. Maybe he or she even had a run-in with the law a time or two. Fast forward to the present day, and you hear that he became a Buddhist priest or she became a Catholic nun. Be honest, you're gonna think, "No f*%#ing way!!!!!!!!" And you, too, just might un-friend them!

I still have a few people—some VERY conservative and some VERY religious—that I stay in touch with by way of Christmas and birthday cards. These friends from my past still think of me as the party girl they knew in the 1980s. The Madonna years......*like a virgin, touched for the very first time, like a vir-ir-ir-ir-gin*......oh, but I digress. Anyway, on my last birthday I received a card about wild girls being rowdy. I happened to be drinking coffee when I opened the envelope and read that—and coffee sprayed all over my kitchen counter! Honestly, anyone who knows me now knows that I couldn't do rowdy these days if it came with a step-by-step manual, a case of Red Bull, and a bottle of amphetamines!! But I haven't seen these folks in thirty-plus years and they remember the wild and rowdy Material Girl wanna-be.

As far as my "whole psychic thing" goes, I'm sure the first thing they said when they found out what I was doing was, "No way!" They're far too conservative and/or religious to say f*%#king. Too, I suspect that they're of the opinion that I burned too many brain cells way back then and that's why now I claim to hear and see things. They think, of course, the poor thing is delusional—and I'm sure I get prayed for a lot! These old friends don't know who I am these days. Of course, I have thirty years' fewer wrinkles in their minds—works for me. You'll probably experience the same with people who knew you way-back-when.

Regardless of how many people un-friend you, you will be able to count on friends who'll be in your life, or who will stay in your life, and who won't disown you—even if they think, *"no f*%#ing way"* or that the psychic stuff is hooey. These people may not share your beliefs, or for that matter even believe you can do what you say you do; nevertheless, they will still be your friends and can be a great support system for you. Frankly, it's good for us to have some non-woo-woos around. Having them makes us have balance in our lives, keeps us grounded, and forces us to engage with others who are non-woo-wooey. Let's be real, all woo-woo all the time makes one just too damned woo-woo! It's a very good thing for birds of different feathers to flock together!

When it comes to who you flock with and who you don't, using a bit of discernment will save you time and energy. Essentially, beware of energetic moochers disguised as friends. These are people who will try to attach themselves to you for one self-serving reason: readings. Free readings at that. This type of person is pretty easy to spot if you're paying attention. There'll be the never-ending barrage of inquiries, such as, *"What do you get around this situation?" "What do you feel about this person?" "What do your guides tell you about what I should do?" "What are you picking up from it?"* or, *"Hey, do a quick reading for me about this thing."* Now, don't get me wrong, I'm more than happy to tune in or do a reading for a friend, as I'm sure that you are too. I mean, what's the point of having this gift if we don't help out our friends with it. But these people I'm talking about aren't real friends. You'll find that the conversations between the two of you will be profoundly one-sided and extraordinarily limited. Ninety-nine percent of your conversations will be centered on whatever is going on in their lives—and they'll want your professional insight about it—as a friend, of course.

At first, being asked for your expert advice may be flattering, but that's the hook. When you catch on that you're just being used, giving your expert advice gets really old really quick. Besides that, it's exhausting when you're persistently being pulled on or when you're consistently asked to make their decisions for them. The solution is to put a stop to that a.s.a.p. and un-hook yourself. What will happen then is that all of a sudden that "friend" will have other things to do, other people to see, other places to be. They'll be gone—and don't feel a bit bad about it! After all, it's not like you're losing a friend because, as they say, you can't lose something you never had. What you might want to do is a happy dance! People like this aren't, never were, never will be, a part of your support system.

The best-case scenario is to not get hooked in the first place. Here's a great example of what I'm talking about. I was invited to a dinner party given by a couple of friends of a friend. I'd never met these folks, but I was told that my reputation preceded me, meaning that they knew I was a psychic, and they were curious. Of course I accepted the invitation, I'm a food whore! From the moment I got to their home, the wife began doting on me and acting as if I was her new BFF. It wouldn't have taken a psychic to see that red flag.

When we sat down to dinner, she immediately began to talk about possibly seeing a tarot card reader that she'd heard of but she *"wasn't sure about that"* and, *"hadn't ever been to one of those"* and, *"not sure what they could tell me"* and, and, and...... No one at the table engaged her in that conversation, although I did catch a lot of looks being exchanged between the other guests, and as the psychic at the table, I can say that it felt very uncomfortable. Since she didn't talk to me directly, I didn't engage either. But I had to applaud her tenacity because she kept on trying. During normal dinner conversation, she turned to me several times with questions like, *"what's your sense on that?* or a, *"how do you feel about that?"* The questions seemed innocent enough, but she sure didn't ask anyone else at the table what their sense was. I usually had a mouth full of food so I'd just shrug my shoulders or I'd say that I didn't know much about whatever the topic was. Actually, I probably came across as a dolt, but I didn't care. The red flags were waving, and my gut screamed, *"Do not engage!"* Therefore, I didn't. I found out a few days later that this woman had a reputation for being manipulative and narcissistic. Alas, we didn't become BFFs—and I never got invited back for dinner.

I'm not saying that you have to be wary of everyone who asks you a question. If they're expressing genuine curiosity about what you do or about being a psychic, good grief, we should welcome that. We're here to educate and enlighten, after all. What I am advocating, though, is that you be an aware and discerning psychic on your own behalf. Learn to recognize the difference between someone who's genuinely interested in you or who has some appreciation for your work, and someone who's trying to hook into you or freeload from you. If mutually profitable questions aren't asked, you might have an energetic moocher on your hands. Certainly, two of the most welcomed questions we could be asked are, "What do you charge?" and "May I have your card?"

Notwithstanding all of the above, who'll be in your life and who'll be a support system will be dictated by the Law of Attraction. That means that you'll inevitably attract other psychics and Lightworkers. In other words, your own kind. That, my friend, deserves a hallelujah, amen, and praise the great Law of Attraction! Everything being equal, there's truly no one else that can understand a psychic more than another psychic. Your immediate family and friends can be great support to you in many, many ways, but unless they themselves are psychics, they can't empathize with you about this work. Other psychics can and will because they experience first-hand the unique challenges that come with the territory. Your spouse or closest friend might be able to relate to you about dealing with a client who's a pain in the neck—after all, they might have a boss who's one of those—but only another psychic will be able to relate to *literally* taking on a pain in the neck from a client!

Only another psychic or energy worker can fully appreciate what an impact psychic/energy work has on the body, mind, and spirit. Knowing that, I'm careful about telling any of my "secular" friends that I'm tired because I had a long day. They'll usually ask how long I worked, to which I'll answer something like, 12-to-5. It's at that point that I get the snicker. But another psychic knows how much energy is expended in those five hours. It's only another psychic who can understand that for five hours I was maintaining my energetic boundaries and protecting my auric field. Another psychic gets it—and will not snicker.

These are your tribal members, these are the co-journeyers in this lifetime that will "get" you, and they can be the most valuable components of your support system. If you don't have these very important people in your life at this time, I'd suggest that you make it your mission to find a few of these kindred spirits. Here's a very short list of some sure ways to meet spiritual kin:

Psychic faires:

Attend or participate in local faires. If you're an attendee, talk to other attendees, strike up conversations with the vendors, get a couple of readings. If you're a participant, walk around before the faire gets started or when you're not busy and introduce yourself to the other participants. You're bound to connect with one or more of them.

As creepy as this might sound, one of the best places at a faire to meet people is in the restroom. (A caveat here: I can only speak first-hand about the ladies' room!) Whether it's while you're waiting in line to use the facilities or at the sink, people tend strike up conversations and dish about the readers, the readings, what's going on around town with the metaphysical community, etc. The bathroom is THE place to go! And, of course, the bathroom is the place to *go*......

Metaphysical Shops:

Make it a point to visit and shop in the stores that are in your area. Become acquainted with the owners and staff. It's a sure thing that if anyone's going to know what's happening in your metaphysical community, it's going to be them. They can be a wealth of information for you. Just remember that they have a business to run, so don't monopolize their time if they're busy.

Okay, here comes a community service announcement: whenever you're in a shop, if possible, make a purchase. Yes, you probably *can* get that book cheaper online, and granted, you already have a drawer full of incense and candles, but it's important that we support these brick-and-mortar shops. They serve as networking central for metaphysicians. You might even say they're a kind of matchmaker for Lightworkers! And in that role, they can play a part in your support system, so return the favor of support.

Classes:

This is a great way to meet people and better yourself. Besides checking with the metaphysical shops, also search the bulletin boards in health food stores, herb shops, rock shops, coffee houses, etc., to see if there are any classes you might enjoy taking. That assures that you're in the company of other like-mindeds. Besides, there's always room for improvement, right?!

On the flip side, if you teach what you know and do, offer your own classes and attract the like-minded to you.

Online:

Find a Meet-Up group or do some online networking. Find a blog you like and engage with it; write a blog and ask for engagement from others.

It doesn't matter how or where you find them, it just matters that you do find your birds-of-a-feather and then flock together—and flock as often as you can! Get together with them to break bread, meet and have coffee, share books, exchange services, or just go out and do something fun. Above all else, be there for one another and be a part of each other's support system.

Last, but not the least, the outer parameter of our support system will consist of those professionals whom we seek out or rely on to help keep ourselves healthy. They're the ones who provide the aid we need in preserving our well-being. They're also the ones who put us back together again when we need it—and some of us need putting back together quite often! In other words, these are going to be our "go to" people—as in we make an appointment and "go to" see them when we need to. But, really, if we're smart, we go to see them **before** we actually need to!

So, let's call this group Team Self-Support. These team members would include practitioners whose healing modalities you benefit from the most, the ones that you have a good rapport with, and those who you don't mind letting into your energy field. Just to name a few, they might be your massage therapist, acupuncturist, psychotherapist, hypnotherapist, reflexologist, hair stylist (hey, looking good is feeling good!), or any other such healer-ists that help you help yourself. Of course, let's not forget, you should have a good psychic on Team Self-Support!

When I began this chapter, I said that Source always has our back. I left it at that because I wanted to focus on the in-body, tactile, can see it with your eyes, hear it with your ears, feel the wind beneath your wings, kind of support. I've subsequently decided that I really can't, in good conscience, leave it at that, but I don't need to write another chapter. I will just very succinctly say:

Never forget that the source of what you see, what you hear, and the wind you feel, is Source. Can I get a HALLELUJAH AMEN?! AMEN!!

*

In the business of being psychic, you will serve as a valuable part of the support systems for many people. You will be part of Team Client. Just don't ever forget that you need support too. You need support for your personal well-being, which translates into the well-being of your business. So then, be Captain of Team Self-Support and call in your best players when you need them!

CHAPTER 11:

YOUR COMPENSATION

There's an old adage that says, "Money is the root of all evil." To that I say, *Money is the root of all evil, my ass!*

Let me make this perfectly clear: YOU DESERVE TO BE PAID FOR YOUR SERVICE. Moreover, you should be paid—and paid WELL—in MONEY, CASH, LEGAL TENDER, CURRENCY, BUCKS, DOLLARS, POUNDS, EUROS, DOUGH, BREAD, MOOLAH, CHA-CHING, or whatever you call it. There are no ifs, ands, or buts about that. There's nothing evil about money and there is unequivocally nothing wrong with you accepting and **expecting** monetary compensation for your services. Receiving money is a fair and appropriate exchange of energies.

The old paradigm has been that it's anathema to talk money concurrently with spiritual work. Even some spiritual practitioners who, in their other lives work in the corporate world, buy into that balderdash. They believe that when they shift gears into spiritual mode the rules of commerce suddenly become objectionable, and that per the old paradigm, it's immoral, sinful, exploitative, sacrilegious even, to do spiritual work and charge for it. It's time for that old paradigm to die—and then to burn the paradigm makers in effigy!

For anyone who sits in judgment of spiritual workers charging a fee for their services, I would like to pose this question to them: *Hey Boob, have you tried to live on this planet without money?* Yeah, I get the whole "we are not of this world" thing, but the reality of it is that we are, here and now, in these bodies, and these bodies have to live *in* this world. Being *in* this world means that we have to, at the very least, take care of our physical needs, i.e., food, shelter, clothing, etc. I don't know about anyone else, but it doesn't make a bit of sense to me to give my abilities away free-of-charge and be emaciated, homeless, and naked! Living in a human body on this planet requires cash, my friends.

These archaic ways of thinking are rooted in religious doctrine which dictates the "vow of poverty" thing. It decrees that one who is blessed by the Divine with spiritual gifts, someone who's doing the Divine's work, should give away these gifts free of charge. Well, that's just a load of crap. I couldn't agree more that these abilities are gifts of the Divine; however, I pose yet another question: Isn't everything a gift from the Divine? To wit:

* Individuals we call surgeons are gifted with a couple of steady hands to perform surgery. So, surgeries should be done for free?

* Those we call singers are gifted with vocal chords to produce beautiful sounds and harmonies. So, CDs and concerts should be free?

* People we call athletes are gifted with extraordinary physical prowess which enables them to play with professional sports teams. So, all sporting events should be free?

* There are those who are gifted with great oratory skills which makes it possible for them to be preachers or motivational speakers. So, there's no need for tithing (ha!) and all self-help seminars should be free?

* Individuals who are gifted with minds for running profitable businesses and making shareholders money……..oh hell, that'll be the day they're giving anything away!

* And on and on and on, ad infinitum.

Each and every one of those examples are Divine gifts. All of those Divine gifts require commitment to and development of the gift on the part of the Divinely gifted individual. All of those Divine gifts will allow someone to make a living for themselves. And some of those livings can be quite lucrative—which is Divine! So why should Lightworkers be the exception to profiting from their Divine gifts?

There's absolutely no good answer for it. Something that's often brought up, which I guess is supposed to be appeasing, is the idea of bartering when it comes to spiritual work. The suggestion is that we should trade a consultation for a chicken, a box of vegetables, a piece of wire-wrapped jewelry, or some other disproportionate thing. I agree that bartering is a great concept IF, and only IF, you want to barter for something you WANT. Bartering works great with your massage therapist, your acupuncturist, your Reiki provider, or another psychic. Bartering can work with the person who has the box of vegetables, as well, but only if those are the vegetables you like, if they're in season, and they're good quality!

Most of the time, however, only money will do because you have to pay it forward. Mortgage lenders, utility companies, gas stations, department stores, etc., expect your payment in either paper or plastic money. Unfortunately, never once have I gone to a grocery store where the cashier offered to trade my groceries for my Divine gift.

I'll also point out that part of being a productive member of society means earning a living (money) and stimulating the economy (again, with money), which makes one a good citizen—I think that's pretty darned Divine, too, wouldn't you agree?! Now, I'm soooo not known for my grasp of economic principles, but I think this scenario would be backed up by fundamental economics:

> Good Citizen provides a service + Good Citizen earns money = happy person.
> Good Citizen spends money in local businesses = happy local businesses.
> Good Citizen and businesses pay taxes to local and federal governments, Good Citizen and businesses maybe not so happy about paying taxes, but = happy local and federal governments, and, Good Citizen and businesses = not in trouble for not paying taxes. Community is able to provide necessary services, such as schools, road maintenance, emergency personnel, parks and recreation services, etc. = most, not all, happy people (some people are just never happy about anything).

> Bottom line: Money is Divinely divine and can do a hell-of-a lot of good. No one should ever begrudge you of making a good living using your Divine gift.

I'm sure it doesn't take a psychic to pick up on my vibes around this topic, does it?! First of all, label me high maintenance if you want to, but being emaciated, homeless, and naked does not appeal to me one little iota! And, trust me, it would be even less appealing to our clients who sit across the table from us—if we then even could afford a table!!

Seriously, though, I do have a strong opinion about the rightfulness of compensation for Lightworkers, and that opinion became profoundly stronger after a negative experience regarding my last book, *How Not To Do A Psychic Reading*—I highly recommend it, it's a great companion to this one (if this were an email there'd be a winking emoticon inserted here!). What happened was that the editor of a publishing company (said publishing company shall remain nameless) called me because he was interested in my book. I was so excited! The book made it through several committees, after which the editor told me that they were pretty much set to publish it, all that was left was the final nod of the Approval Committee, which he said was "a mere formality." But it got shot down in that meeting. Why? Because I simply *alluded* to charging money for readings. I merely mentioned it. It wasn't a full chapter on compensation or even a topic that I discussed in any length—unlike here and now.

What was incomprehensible about the rejection is that the heart of the book centers on why and how psychics should practice ethically and work in integrity. The heart, unfortunately, wasn't enough to override some archaic dogma they were attached to. Actually, their stance had more than a little irony and a whole lot of hypocrisy attached to it, if you ask me—and that's not sour grapes talking. The proof is what I've seen on their website and on bookstore shelves. In neither of those places could I find any of the Divinely-inspired, spiritually-themed books published by this company being given away free-of-charge. I'd also venture a guess that those on the final approval committee, those that were opposed to charging a fee for a service, were not donating their Divine gifts. Again, I'm just venturing guesses here.

Psychics should prosper from using their gifts—and shouldn't have to argue a case for it. One thing that's inarguable is that being profitable shouldn't be an unfamiliar state or lifestyle for psychics, since money and success are on a client's top three list ninety-nine percent of the time (the other two being relationships and health). When clients come in for a reading, not only are they looking for insight into their financial situations, but they're also wanting advice on how to achieve more abundance in their lives. Most psychics are able to offer that by means of recommending a good book or two on manifesting abundance, a.k.a., money. However, if we're dressed in tatters, looking hungry, living under a bridge, and thumbing a ride, would we really look like we know of a good book on how to create success and prosperity?! Would we really be able to look the client in the eye and say, *Yes, this is a great book, it works!?* I should say not!! Moreover, if the book endorsement is coming from a vow of poverty personified, I bet the authors would appreciate their books not being mentioned!!

I've just presented the case to the world that psychics, energy workers, healers, any and all Lightworkers, should be compensated—and compensated handsomely—for their Divine gifts. Unfortunately, there are still spiritual people that need convincing that receiving payment in cash money is a good thing and that it's in Divine order. So, I'll continue to stump the money issue.

Spiritual workers aren't alone when it comes to issues with money. Everyone has a dysfunctional relationship with money in some way or another. It doesn't matter who they are, whether it's being a ninety-nine percenter or even if they're among the one-percent uber-super wealthy. Money issues tend to be universal. The issue can be in how one views money, whether one believes they deserve money, in how money is handled, basically, one's relationship with money. Unfortunately, the issue with money for Lightworkers can be worse, especially if they've bought into the bull-shenanigans like how it's "un-spiritual" to capitalize on their gifts, that spiritual people shouldn't desire to be rich (or have desires at all), that the riches they seek are the ones awaiting in Heaven (barf), or that making and/or having money will somehow make them a bad person, or, get this one, if you accept money for using your gifts you'll lose them. GIVE ME A BREAK! NONE OF THAT IS TRUE!! NOT ONE LITTLE BITTY BIT OF IT!!! Therefore, when you're asked about your readings, say clearly and confidentially something like: *I charge $$$, and I take cash, check, and credit cards.* Another thing, if a client asks if you accept tips...... I *know* I really don't have to finish that one, right?!

If you're called to this work, and if you put your heart and soul into it, you owe it to yourself to allow your Self to prosper. Let go of the lies of any crusty old dogma and perverted programming. Charge a fee for the energy you're giving out and joyfully accept money-energy in return. Of course, if you insist on giving your time and energy away for free, or really do prefer to barter for a box of vegetables, who am I to suggest otherwise? Just remember, enlightenment doesn't come cheap—the electric company wants payment in dollars for it.

Now that's it's been established that compensation and money are Divine, what should a psychic entrepreneur charge for their services? Well, the simple answer is: whatever the psychic entrepreneur thinks they deserve. But let's take that beyond the simple answer.

The most important thing to take into account when setting your consultation fee is that the amount of money you charge your clients should be a fair exchange for the service you provide them. Here are a few considerations for determining a fee:

- Your experience. Specifically, how long you've been doing readings. Similar to any other occupation, compensation should be commensurate with the length of time you've been doing the work. The longer you've been doing it, the more experience you bring to the table. The more experience you have, the more you should earn.

- Your proficiency. Basically, that means the range and scope of what you can deliver, such as the *who, what, when, where, how.* Do you consider yourself a "general practitioner," in that you cover a bit of all aspects of the client's life? Or are you more of a "specialist," whereby you pretty much devote the entire session to one or two specific areas, i.e., health, past lives, investments, communicating with those that have passed on, or animal communication.

- Your credentials. In corporate terms, it's the stuff you'd put on a resume to make yourself look good. In this case, it would be any and all training and/or classes you've taken, as well as any training, classes, or lectures you've given. If you've written a book(s), have had articles published in trade magazines or online websites, or if you have a blog, all will add to your credentials. Anything and everything that gives you some name recognition can be factored into setting a fee.

There is no one-fee-fits-all, however. If you're putting your shingle out for the first time, or if you've moved to a new location and are establishing your practice anew, before setting your fee you may wish to gauge what the average rate is in the area. As always, the go-to place for that kind of information is your local metaphysical store. Find out what they're charging for readings, although I've found that they typically charge less than psychics in private practice do. Then, check out the websites of other psychics to see what they do and what their rates are—and don't overlook *how* they charge. By that I mean if it's by the half-hour, by the hour, or as some do, psychic hotlines, for instance, by the minute. Then, with that information in hand, compare what you know and what you do, and set your fee.

Think long-term when you're trying to establish yourself. If you're just starting out or you're a newcomer to the area, your objective is to grow your business, so you might consider charging a little less for a while than someone who's been in business for a long time. Something else to consider is offering an introductory price or an initial consultation discount. These are great win-win ways to introduce yourself to potential clients. It's a fact, when savvy shoppers get something on sale that they really, really like and it's really, really good quality and it really, really works for them, they'll really, really continue to buy it even when it's no longer on sale. Many of your clients will be savvy shoppers—really! Once they know what you can do and how you can help them, they WILL come back to you and they WILL pay you what you're worth.

In this chapter, I've talked on and on about receiving; however, I would be remiss if I ended this chapter without mentioning the counterpart to receiving, which is giving. Assuming that all our needs are met, all the bills are paid, and that we're not emaciated, homeless, and naked, it's incumbent upon us to give back. We call it tithing, seeding, flowing, alms, sharing the wealth, paying it forward, and so on and so forth. Each of us will have our own reasons to give, such as we give because it's a dictate of our faith, we believe it's a Universal principle, or we like the release of the endorphins that give us a "helper's high" (that's a real thing, look it up). Regardless of what we call it or the intention behind it, giving is just a plain ol' nice thing to do!

Giving is also easy—just pick your cause and then pick a charity. Charities make giving easy because they always welcome money. Charities don't ascribe to crusty outdated dogma so they don't think money is evil! If your schedule permits, volunteering your time is a great alternative—time is money, after all. Pick an organization whose good work is near and dear to your heart and support it in whatever fashion works best for you. Give and give generously. Give away as much of your time, money, and your gifts as possible.

Support your favorite charity by donating your services. Most charitable organizations hold fund-raising events throughout the year and, depending on the organization and the function, would welcome having a psychic do readings at one or more of those events—especially at Halloween. If doing something like that appeals to you, offer to be their psychic. In addition to the fund-raiser itself, silent auctions often are a part of those events. Consider donating a gift certificate for a reading.

It's all about the giving and being altruistic, for sure, but just an aside, any venue where you can showcase your abilities is a great way to promote your Divine services. Hey, there's nothing wrong in finding a win-win in a situation! Besides, your self-promotion will lead to new clients which means more business, and more compensation for you, which allows you to give more to the charity. See, everybody's happy—and that's so Divine!!

Life is meant to be filled with richness for all of us. Richness of love, richness of happiness, richness of joy, and yes, most definitely, richness in the form of bling and cashola! If we're to fulfill our duties as being a messenger of Spirit, the voice of Infinite Intelligence, the gofer for God, we need to eat, be clothed, have a place to live, and, without any doubt, afford Starbucks.

*

In the business of being psychic, your business should prosper. You should prosper. Contrary to Dark Age doctrine, money is actually the root of all that is Divine. And you can take that to the bank!

CHAPTER 12:

YOUR CONTRACTUAL OBLIGATIONS

I didn't consult with Gallop Poll on this, but I think that it's safe to say that the majority of professional psychics are in private practice. It's even safer to say that the average mainstream corporation doesn't hire on-staff psychics. I'm sure there are exceptions to that, just as sure as I am that Bigfoot exists—and I am sure of that. But those companies are the anomalies, and I bet they do the government thing and keep that "department" top secret! Law enforcement agencies may hire psychics to assist in investigations, but even then, they probably hire those psychic detectives as independent consultants, not as on the payroll employees.

In whatever manner your services are contracted, whether you're in private practice, you're a sub-contractor or consultant, or you're an actual employee in some anomalous corporation in a top-secret department, you'll have contractual obligations. How well you fulfill your obligations can make or break your business.

Let's begin with a very sacred, albeit unwritten, contract you enter into with each and every client you work with. Your part of that contract stipulates that you'll provide your service to the best of your ability in conjunction with Infinite Intelligence. It means you'll conduct yourself as a professional and you'll treat your clients with the utmost dignity and respect. It also means that you'll be fully present for them: physically (being on time), mentally (not preoccupied with anything else), and psychically (that comes naturally).

For your client's part, they agree to offer their appreciation of your time and gift by financial remuneration, which is a fancy way of saying that they pay you money, which may be tendered in the form of cash, check, or credit card. That remuneration then leads to a significant obligation you have, which is to report your earnings to Uncle Sam. We don't exactly have a contractual obligation with this Uncle, it's more like a "hand it over or we'll shoot" understanding.

I don't do my own taxes. If I did, I'd probably be wearing an orange jumpsuit and would be the girlfriend of someone named Big Bertha. So, let me be very clear, I *can't* and *don't* and *won't* and *am not* giving any kind of tax advice! What I am advising is that you keep really good records of your income and remember that you have to pay taxes on that income. Whatever money you personally deposit into your bank account, or what Square sends to your bank account, or whatever money goes into your PayPal account, is considered income. You'll be obligated to pay taxes on that income. Let me reiterate: if it's deposited into your bank account, checking or savings, it must be reported as income.

I emphasize this because a massage therapist I once knew got into very hot water with the IRS because she thought that only the checks that she deposited were considered income. She deposited all the cash she made into her bank account, but she, in her words, "didn't think cash counted." When you deposit cash you've earned, know that you're obligated to pay income tax on that cash. Although, rumor has it that cash that doesn't get deposited doesn't count......that's what I hear anyway.......but I am unequivocally NOT spreading that rumor.

If you're an actual employee, say, of a metaphysical shop or of a government agency that "doesn't exist," then you'll be on their payroll and will receive a W-2 Form at the end of the year. If that's the case, then there's little to no fuss—and no fudging—in doing your taxes.

Overall, though, most of us are in private practice and/or contract out our services as freelancers or independent contractors. If you have a formal contract, say for instance, with a metaphysical store or a law enforcement agency, the entity contracting your services will most likely provide you with a 1099 Form at the end of the year. Why is that important to know? Because it means that they had to report to the IRS how much they paid you—and you had better report that much too! Unless, of course, they paid you in cash and you didn't deposit that cash. I'm just sayin'.

Organizers of metaphysical faires typically require that the participants sign a contract with them. These contracts are pretty standard and, basically, they're intended to set out guidelines for the event and to release themselves from any liability, like maybe someone hated their reading so much that they try to sue the organizers, or some other far-fetched thing. But most importantly, the contract is designed to absolve the organizers from any lack of financial reporting on behalf of the participants. It makes the participants solely responsible for reporting their earnings from the faire.

We satisfy our tax obligations because we're good, law-abiding, honest citizens. Yeah, yeah, sure, but let's be honest, we pay up because if we don't the IRS will come after our asses! On the other hand, the contracts that we have with our clients, whether they're written or unwritten, spoken or unspoken, don't have to be fulfilled under penalty of the law, but to build your business, upholding your end will assure your success.

Let's then take a look at a few other situations where you'd have an obligation:

In metaphysical shops:

If you're not actually an employee of the shop, some shop owners will want some sort of basic written agreement between the two of you. These are meant to generally set forth what they'll pay you or what percentage they'll take from the readings you'll do. It would also designate the days you'll do readings, and any particular protocol they have for their readers. Other shops won't do anything at all in writing, but you'll be expected to uphold your part of what you agreed upon.

Partnering with the right metaphysical store can be a great boon to your business, particularly if you're trying to get yourself established. By virtue of its physical presence alone, a storefront will attract many more people than you probably could, or could afford to, independently. Shops draw people in through the classes they offer, from the services they provide, and by stocking the metaphysical needs of the community. And, in essence, you can piggy-back on them. You can also garner more credibility when your services are featured under the umbrella of a business. Clients tend to feel a certain surety about the readers that shop owners employ in their establishments. I guess their logic is that a store owner won't bring in a sucky psychic! But if all that wasn't enough, there's an added bonus to being associated with a shop, and that is that the staff will go out of their way to promote you to any and all customers who walk through the door—even to the customer who only comes in for a pack of incense!

Of course, what the staff is doing is pimping you out! After all, the more readings you do, the more money they make from their percentage of the readings. The more in demand you are, the more money they make because more customers are coming in. Basically, the more readings you do, the more money you and the store will make. That's a good deal! Actually, that's pimping at its finest!!

Something to keep in mind when you're working in such venues is you may be an independent contractor, but don't take the "independent" part too far. When you work in a metaphysical store it helps to have the same temperament and cooperative spirit as if you were playing on a sports team. In other words, it's all about the team. If you've contracted with a shop, you're a part of that team. Nothing more, nothing less.

How many readers a store will have in-house, and how they feature those readers, depends on the store's volume of business, the availability of quality readers, and the owner's goals for their store. A little shop in a small town might just have one or two psychics that they rotate. However, a larger store in a big city may have a different psychic every day, or even several at any given time. Regardless of how many psychics there are in a store, each one of them is an equal component in the larger whole. Meaning that it's a team, everyone has their place on the team, and each place is equally important.

I've been in and around metaphysical shops for many, many years and, unfailingly, there would always be *that* psychic who would make their entrance into a store with a prima donna attitude. *Whatever*, I'd think, and roll my eyes (because I do that kind of tacky thing). What I couldn't *whatever* away was that they'd treat the staff like servants—their servants no less. That's just not cool. Some store owners would tolerate a psychic behaving badly, some didn't.

If you're ever fortunate enough to partner-up with a metaphysical store, be sure to respect the staff and know that it's not in their job descriptions to be in servitude to the readers. Their primary responsibility is to serve the store's customers. Just as it's the reader's primary responsibility to serve the store's customers, a.k.a., their own clients. Using the sports team analogy again, if you piss off your teammates—and especially if you piss off the team owner—one too many times, no matter how talented you are, you WILL find yourself being a free agent!

Actually, it takes very little to stay in the good graces of a store's staff. All you have to do is follow through on what your agreement with them is, as well as be considerate of them. Basically, it's practicing common courtesy. For instance, say you committed to being their reader five days a week. Then, guess what? You need to show up five days a week. If for some reason you find that those days don't work for you, renegotiate the agreement—don't just not show up. The store owner has a business to run, customers to serve, and a reputation to maintain. No part of their concerns should be wondering whether or not their psychic is going to make an appearance. Of course, the unexpected happens—even to a psychic, who would think? Undoubtedly, there'll be occasions, like illness or some family emergency, when you'll need time off or won't be able to make it in. On those occasions, do your best to give the staff as much notice as humanly possible so that they can get a replacement in there for you. (And yes, as crushing as it is to hear, you can be replaced!). That's part of your obligation to them. If you're a no show, no call, no text, no email, you will wind up being a *no more* and your temporary replacement will end up being permanent! Oh, but of course there are times when it's acceptable to be a no-show, say, because of the fury of nature—floods, tornadoes, mountain lion attack, meteor strike, and/or the poles shifting.

Otherwise, show up and show up on time. What you do have control over—when stuff is happening—is informing the staff as to what your situation is, giving them an E.T.A., and keeping them updated. If you're being delayed because of a traffic accident, road construction, or your home is surrounded by hungry bears, call or text the shop immediately. Be considerate of the store and your waiting clients' time. After all, you're not the only one being inconvenienced by traffic or hungry bears.

Occasional lateness is understandable, but there's no good excuse for chronic lateness. Unless you consider rudeness a good excuse. It may seem that being late a mere five or ten minutes is inconsequential, but it's really not. Let's consider the consequence of those few minutes. Besides those five or ten minutes late in getting there, most likely you'll then need another five or ten minutes to set up. And, let's be real here, you'll probably then need to use the restroom. That's, give or take, twenty minutes of lateness that becomes the burden of the **staff**. It falls on their shoulders to make your excuses—AND APOLOGIES—to your clients that are waiting. It also throws off the rest of the day's scheduling for readings. Once again, that burden of explaining and apologizing to YOUR clients falls to the store representatives standing at the counter. Therefore, if you committed to begin the sessions at 10 a.m., consider getting there by 9:45, or earlier if you need more time to set up or more time in the restroom. In that way, by 10, you can be A.I.C. (ass in chair) and READY to work!

There are a couple of extra courtesies that I'd like to suggest here. I doubt that they're in your contract with the shop—and I guarantee that they won't be in your job description—so you're certainly not obligated in any way to do them, but if Spirit moves, consider a few above-and-beyond niceties.

The first thing is to lend a hand. Even if you only use the reading room once a week, consider tidying it up. I'm not suggesting that you should break out the vacuum and furniture polish! I'm saying that if you walk into the space and there's an overflowing trash can or ashy incense burner, you could empty the can or clean the burner. Yes, it's a little over and above, but when you're in the store and using the space, why not treat it as if it was your own? You may not have any influence on the setup or décor of the space, but you can do your part to maintain its cleanliness. Even more, you would be giving the staff a helping hand. Without question, it's not your responsibility to clean up after the reader who used the room before you, but you're using the room at that moment, and its condition at that moment is a direct reflection on you. At the very least, pick up after yourself so that tomorrow's reader is not looking at the remnants of what you had for lunch today.

Store owners and their staff stay very busy with customers and with keeping the store running. That includes attracting clientele for the psychics (you) to make money. They're also providing and maintaining a location for the psychics (again, you) to do readings and make money. Even though it is their responsibility to keep the store clean, with all that they do for the psychics (still you), occasionally a trash can gets overlooked. So, empty it. My thought is that I'd rather dump the can than have my Virgo or Libra clients focused on the trash and thinking, *Geez, why don't they empty that thing?* Or worse, *What's that smell?*

Another thing to take upon yourself is welcoming your clients. The staff can't—and shouldn't—be expected to bring people to you. They're busy in the store serving customers. Even if it's a super-slow day, they've got other things on their to-do list like restocking shelves, taking inventory, placing orders, rearranging displays, cleaning the restroom, answering phones, booking appointments for the psychics, to name a few. So once you get settled in the space, and when you've made it yours for the day, go out front to meet and greet your clients. Welcome them as if you were welcoming them into your home or into your private office. Greeting your clients will serve to assuage any nervousness or apprehension they may have, plus, you'll be making a great first impression. After a warm hello, escort them back to the space for the session. You'd be amazed at how something so simple can set the right tone for the reading.

While still on the topic of contracting with metaphysical stores, there's a gray area that I'd like to address. It's a dilemma that faces a psychic who's partnering with a store, while also maintaining a private practice. The issue is that sometimes readers are tempted to steal clients away from the store. This can be a bit of a slippery slope issue. Typically, metaphysical stores don't make their psychics sign a "non-compete" agreement, so, technically, you're not obligated in any way to not steal clients. But ethics are another matter.

Should you find yourself in such a dilemma, my suggestion is that you weigh the facts of your situation, and then do what your heart chakra dictates and what your conscience allows. The general facts are that, on one hand, a store will take a percentage of the readings you do. Unless it's a very unfair split, they're more than entitled to their cut—that's a fact. They earn it for all the reasons aforementioned. On the other hand, your private consultation fees are one-hundred percent yours to keep. Nobody's taking a percentage, you might charge more privately, and it's all going into your pocket. Sounds like a no-brainer but allow me offer my humble opinion for your consideration.

First of all, the store shouldn't be viewed as a competitor. After all, you've been professional partners, business co-creators, and teammates. Of course, if they're abusive to you, if they beat you black and blue, or they take ninety-five percent of your earnings, then go ahead and undercut the bastards! But if that's the situation, you're probably not working in a metaphysical store, but in a sweat shop instead! So, although the financial incentive may be tempting to lure the store clientele into seeing you privately, that's just......slimy.

The same holds true if you work for psychic hotlines or any other phone consultation service. Most of those have a non-compete clause, a.k.a., no stealing clients, in their contracts, and you'd better believe that they have ways of knowing whether or not you're honoring that clause. So you'd better think long and hard before you'd consider stealing any clients off the line. Be aware that when you're found out, your services will be terminated without any further ado. And then what will you *a-do*?

I've got nothing to remedy slimy, but if someone thinks that they need to steal clients, or steal anything for that matter, it's a good bet that they don't trust in the Universe to provide for them. I could speak endlessly from my deep KNOWING, not just trusting, of how the Universe provides for us and how abundance abounds, but that would be another book entirely—and that's unnecessary because there's an *abundance* of great books written by an *abundance* of great teachers—a handful of which are listed at the end of this book in Recommended Reading. What I can do is assure you that if you're a good psychic and if you embrace and trust the Universal laws of prosperity and the Law of Attraction, you'll always have plenty of clients seeking you out—in both the store and in private. There's more than enough of everything for everyone. The bottom line then is that there's no need to steal clients away from a store.

Nevertheless, from time to time you'll have a store client call you for a reading on a day other than your day at the store. They might have a time-sensitive opportunity, or they may need to make an immediate life-altering decision. No matter what the situation is, your client believes that they can't—or just don't want to—wait until it's your day at the store. Note that there's a very discernable difference between a scenario like this one, where the client is "stalking" you, and one where you'd solicit a client away from the store. Very simply, the former is you going, *pssst, why don't you come see me privately but don't tell anyone from the store*; the latter is the client calling you and saying, *I want to see you, I don't want to wait*, or, *I want to see you and I don't want to go to the store.* Although, if a client calls and says, *I want to see you because I have a crush on you*, well then, that's just creepy. I'd make sure I see them solely within the safety of the store—with the reading room door wide open!

These are NOT unusual situations. It stands to reason that clients are gonna wanna stick with those psychics that they've developed a relationship with and who know what's going on with them. Those clients will contact *you* because it's *you* that they want and only *you* will do. In these instances then, if they can't wait until your day at the store, there's nothing unethical about setting up a private appointment with them. Since they're gonna wanna be exclusively yours, you certainly can't be accused of cheating on the store! The client, on the other hand, well, maybe.

Before you set up an appointment with a client under these circumstances, make it clear to them right up-front what you personally charge. If your fee is the same as what the store charges for a reading, or if you're going to give the client the store rate, it's a non-issue and doesn't need to be addressed. Otherwise, if your private fee is more than the store's, inform them right then and there that there's a price difference. Don't wait until the reading is over and then spring it on them. Understand, it's more than likely that a difference in fees never occurred to them—and then it's more than likely that they won't appreciate the surprise! After a client knows that you charge more and recognizes that they've gotten you as a "bargain" all along, they can make an informed decision about whether to book an appointment with you privately or else wait to see you on your regular day in the store.

Metaphysical faires and other events:

If you're invited to participate in a psychic faire, or any event for that matter, there are a few things to consider before you agree to sign on.

The first thing to understand is that the organizers of events will be counting on you to keep your commitment to show up. You wouldn't think that this is an issue that has to be addressed, but it does because no-shows happen. Readers, as well as healers, energy workers, and vendors, will agree to participate and then just not show up—even if they paid for their space. I guess if someone has never organized a big event, they can't appreciate the incredible amount of work it takes to pull off.

There's a hell-of-a lot of planning that goes into making these things successful for everyone involved. An unfortunate result of a no-show is that there's a gap in the layout that was planned, which then has to be quickly reconfigured. The worst part about it is that someone else could've filled that slot—and they could've expanded their business. A no-show is a big deal. If you care about your reputation, as well as about being invited to participate in some future event, don't be a no-show.

If you've committed to participate, then also commit to show up on time. It's not appropriate, nor is it professional, to be disruptive to the readers on either side of you by barreling in late. Be a good neighbor! Plan to get to the faire in ample time to set up your space, use the restroom, meet your neighbors, and be A.I.C. (ass in chair) and ready to begin readings when the doors open to the public.

Abide by whatever rules the organizers laid out. Depending on the venue, a pretty universal restriction is no incense, scented candles, or sprays. If that's a rule for your event, go scentless. I've actually seen participants get quite indignant about not being able to have a lit candle on their table or spritz their sprays. What some people may not understand is that there are two very good reasons for these restrictions:

1—Municipal fire codes usually dictate no open flames in public buildings; and,

2—Because there are a lot of people who are sensitive, if not highly allergic, to strong scents.

Think what it would be like if every participant burned or sprayed something. The room would be congested with scents, creating much nasal congestion! To restrict the scents just makes *sense*.

A request that will probably be in a contract is:

TURN OFF YOUR CELLPHONE! TURN OFF YOUR CELLPHONE!! TURN OFF YOUR CELLPHONE!!!
Oh yeah, one more thing, in no uncertain terms: TURN OFF YOUR CELLPHONE!!!!!

Please. Thank you.

The bluntest reason is that no one should be subjected to your ringing cellphone. Expounding on that, when a paying client sits down in front of a psychic for a reading, they shouldn't be interrupted by the psychic's phone—and the paying client sure as hell shouldn't be expected to sit there and watch the psychic dig around for their phone in order to turn it off! Or worse, to answer it!! Too, when other readers are doing their jobs and are tuning into other realms, they shouldn't be subjected to a blast of a hallelujah chorus, giggling squirrels, some old disco music, or some other buffoonish ringtone—or even a very happy tune like mine, which is "*Happy*" by Pharrell Williams!!

Last, but not least, no faire participant or attendee should be disturbed or distracted by your conversations. Admit it, we all tend to increase the decibel of our voices when we're on our cellphones. Make and take all your calls outside the venue, unless it's an absolute emergency—like maybe you left home early while your mate was still sleeping, and you forgot to leave a note about the mountain lion stalking your property. Barring any emergencies, give your complete and undivided attention to the task at hand, which is to astound people with your gifts, give them much-needed insight, make some new clients, and have fun! Just remember that it's an obligation to be respectful and considerate of the other readers.

One last thing to keep in mind about faire participation. Recognize that in order to have a successful faire it takes everyone coming together doing their part in harmony with each other. It's very much like musicians in a symphony orchestra. Although each one is playing a different instrument, they're all playing the same concert and all following the same conductor. So, respect what the other faire participants bring to the collective event. The public will feel the good vibes. Then, the next time it's advertised, they'll want to attend and bring their friends. That means more clientele for you!

Another thing organizers may ask of you is to stay until the faire shuts down. And, if you agreed to do that, then stay until the faire shuts down. Depending on how an event is going, that indeed may be a little bit of a challenge. Have no doubt, there'll be faires where the attendance is so low that you'll be bored out of your mind—and we all know that the mind is a terrible thing to waste! So why endure until the bitter end? Because if you agreed to stay until the faire shuts down, then stay until the faire shuts down. Honor your commitment.

If it's your very first faire, if you're new in town, or if you're just beginning your practice, you can count on having some slow time. But rest assured, you won't be wasting your time. You'll be proving yourself to be reliable and someone who's true to their word. If you bail out, the organizers will, in all *fairness*, not invite you back to any future events they sponsor.

Frankly, sometimes being idle isn't so bad. When I was a faire newbie, I'd feel like a pound puppy. I'd sit at my table looking up at the people walking by, just hoping that one of them would choose to sit down in front of me. Then, when one of them did decide to sit in the chair across from me, the pound puppy feeling would go away, only to be replaced with the terror of, *Oh dear God in heaven, this person is sitting in front of me, now I've got to do a reading for them! I don't know if I'm ready for this. What if I can't read for them? And...and...and...* But that was me (I had issues!).

Regardless of whether you're a busy puppy or not, remain A.I.C. as much as possible until the faire is over. Bring a book, your iPad, some knitting, crossword puzzles, or anything else that can occupy your time; something that can be put aside quickly, because you never know (even if you are psychic) when someone's going to be drawn to you and will sit down at your table. A.I.C. can pay off, but it might take all day. You'd be surprised how many people—meaning potential new clients—show up near or right at closing time.

Finally, a gesture of appreciation would go a long way. As I said previously, putting on an event takes an incredible amount of time and effort. With that in mind, consider taking a moment to thank the organizers. You might do that either before you leave or else shoot them an email afterward expressing your appreciation. We all know first-hand how good a little appreciation feels. Pay it forward!

Fundraisers:

Participating in a fundraiser is a fantastic opportunity to give back. If you agreed to volunteer your service to them, then it's your obligation to show up for them. Even if it's not a paying "gig," and regardless of whether or not you signed an actual contract, an obligation is an obligation.

Law Enforcement:

I'm not familiar with any of the specifics contained in contracts between law enforcement agencies and psychics, but as with any confidentiality agreement, there's sure to be a standard, non-negotiable, no exception clause about discretion. Since I don't know what the exact legalese would be, I'll paraphrase. I suppose it would go something like: *PSYCHIC DOES NOT BLAB! Said Psychic doesn't have a right to remain silent, said Psychic has an absolute, binding obligation to be silent. In the event that said Psychic does shoot off his/her mouth, said Psychic's ass will be in deep doo-doo.* Or something along those lines.

If you're a psychic that contracts to work with law-enforcement, you will be obligated to be zip-lipped about any case that you work on. That means that you do not discuss with ANYONE what you know about a particular case, even if it's been on the news. It's not out of the realm of possibility that what you leak may get back to a victim or a victim's family, which can then cause more pain for them. Another concern is that leaks regarding a case can be potentially damaging to the prosecution of that case. Most of all, a professional psychic should be the epitome of discretion.

Whatever kind of agreement you make, whether you sign a formal written contract, make a verbal commitment, or simply promise with an informal handshake, it's crucial to honor any and all agreements. Be someone who is true to your word. For certain, the success of your business relies heavily upon your talents. But you can also be certain that when you prove yourself to be a responsible and reliable professional, you'll be one much sought after psychic. Can we agree on that?

*

In the business of being psychic, making good on any and all of your contractual obligations is just as important as how psychic you are.

*

CHAPTER 13:

YOUR BUSINESS

You're the boss. You call the shots. This is your business. True, it's not a typical kind of business; nonetheless, it is a business, and it's important to treat it as such, from its inception, to maintaining it, and on to the expansion of it.

For the most part, psychic counseling practices fall into one of these categories:

1. These are psychics who do readings "for entertainment purposes only." No, they don't sing and dance Spirit's messages, they read for friends and family strictly for fun and totally free of charge. The kitchen table is usually where the readings are done.

2. These psychics will do readings for people outside their immediate F&F circle for a little extra cash or a barter of some kind. Indeed, these folks will accept a box of vegetables or a chicken! These readings are usually done from someone's kitchen table as well.

3. Some psychics exclusively do consultations from metaphysical shops, work on psychic hotlines, and/or do readings only at psychic faires.

4. Those who've built up a sizable practice and maintain an office, either in their home or one rented in a commercial building. The readings would be either their primary source of income or a substantial portion of it;

5. Then there are the few psychics who have made it in the "big-time." They're the ones who've published best-selling books or have appeared on radio, television, reality shows, or had their own show. Some are also known for being the psychics to the stars—and I mean Hollywood, not the constellations! As far as having any business advice for this group, I've got nothin', but I'd sure welcome whatever advice they'd be willing to offer! *Hey, call me!!*

But I've got a lot of somethin' if your practice falls into one of the first four groups. This chapter is chock-full of suggestions to establish yourself as a professional, as well as taking your existing business to the next level. Every bit of advice offered is practical, feasible, tried and true, and for the most part, easy to do. What may be difficult is deciding how much you want to grow your practice. As they say: be careful what you wish for!

If you currently work from your kitchen table, are you ready to create—and commit to—a real practice?

If you already have a moderate client base, are you willing to invest the time and energy into expanding it?

Are you shooting for the big-time? If you are, understand what all that entails. And by the way, if you're going big and should get your own reality show, I'd sure appreciate a shout-out!!

One of the most important influences for your practice will be for you to acknowledge that it is a genuine business, and then give yourself permission to treat it as a business. As I mentioned in the chapter, "Your Compensation," spiritual workers sometimes have a difficult time with the practicalities of commerce. They worry that they'd lose their focus, become too materialistic, or it'll somehow ruin them. But a business is just like any other thing, like money, guns, drugs, Pitbulls, etc., it's not the *thing* that's dangerous or tainted, it's who's in control of the thing. Rest assured, if you're a good psychic with good intentions and have a desire to be in service to the world, it's the right control. So, be a business.

Consider becoming a legal entity. While it's certainly possible to conduct business under your own name, there are advantages to becoming a legal entity, which means registering as a "DBA." Instead of me trying to explain what that means, and surely botching it up and confusing the hell out of you, I've taken the following from www.dbaform.com:

> DBA, short for "doing business as," is a formal declaration that an individual, company or organization is conducting business under a different name. DBA's are also commonly referred to as fictitious business names, assumed business names and trade names. All these terms mean the same thing.

Typically, businesses are officially created when registered under the owner's name. When this occurs, the owners often choose a name for the business and register a DBA to make it official. If your business is registered under your name and you intend to conduct business under a different name, you must file a DBA.

DBA's need to be filed so business owners can use the name in contracts, open bank accounts, write and deposit checks with that business name. It also discourages competitors from using your name or a similar one.

There may be restrictions on your DBA choice. For example, some states may not allow it to reference a geographical location unless you're located there. If you have decided on a business name and find out that someone else already has that name, you may still be able to register it if you are in a different industry or trade.

Filing a DBA is a good initial step in formally establishing your business. And, you'll only need to renew it every 4 to 5 years, depending on your state. There are no yearly fees. If you want to cancel your DBA, simply don't renew it.

There are myriad benefits to being a legal and licensed small business—that is, if licensing is necessary in your state. Not the least of the benefits is how much "stuff" you can legally write-off, which we'll cover later in this chapter. First, you've got to name your business.

As with any "newborn" you have to decide on a name for your newly born business. Since it's your baby, you can call it whatever your little heart desires. You could simply use your name or you can use a pseudonym, your stage name, pen name, what you call your alter ego, or an alias. Otherwise, make up a name. If you're so inclined, attach "& Company" to the name—only you need to know that your "Company" is your non-physical associates! You can call your business anything you wish, just so long as the name isn't already taken. To find out if the name is in use already, do a search with your local city or county records office of the businesses registered. If the name is available, it's yours for the taking, then register it.

What I'd strongly suggest is that you give some serious thought to what you call your business. Remember, the name of your business represents you. It introduces you to the public and may be a potential client's first impression of you. Keep in mind that if your name is too pretentious or weird, you risk putting people off. And a too obvious or ubiquitous name, say, *Psychic Your First Name*, make people say, *yeah, yeah, sure, aren't you all.* Find your perfect fit by test driving a few names. Bounce several names off your friends and family. Ultimately, you'll know you've found it when it FEELS right when you hear it said out loud. Essentially, it'll be the right fit when it FEELS like you!

After you've decided on what you're calling your business, check online with your local municipality for the requirements to set up your DBA. This part is critical. Not only is every state different, like gross receipts tax for instance, but different cities have different requirements. On the other hand, some cities will have no requirements at all, except that you pay your taxes.

Depending on where you live, you might be required to obtain a business license. If that's the case, get the license. After all, the more legit you are, the more legit you are. Of course, there's a nominal fee, and the license will usually have to be renewed on a yearly basis. But the good news is that license fees are tax-deductible!

Once you get your business license (if applicable), put it in a frame and display it prominently in your workplace. You can tack it to the wall, but that diminishes the professionalism a bit. Displaying the license is usually a requirement of the city, but there's a real benefit to your business. When a client sees a license, it lends credibility to you. There's a psychological, almost subliminal, boost to your credibility when you have an "official" document validating you as "legal." Although you may be incredibly talented, and that's what your credibility should be based on, you will only be perceived and respected as a "real" business if you have "papers." I'm certainly not saying that it's right, it's just the way it is. It's a matter of how people perceive things. And, let's face it, we all have our own preconceived perceptions.

For instance, imagine that your car needs some work, and you have the choice of taking it to Joe the mechanic guy who works on cars in the garage behind his house, or going to Joe the mechanic who owns Joe's Auto Repair Shop. If you didn't know either Joe, or didn't know anyone who had been to either Joe, in all likelihood you'd take your vehicle to Joe's Auto Repair because he's the one who has the establishment and who has the business license—the official document—on his wall. Your decision would undoubtedly be based on the fact that this Joe is, in the eyes of the local government, a sanctioned "real" business. Ol' Joe who's working out of his garage may be a master mechanic with more experience, he could have all the right tools, and he might even be a nicer guy, but he just doesn't give the appearance of legitimacy. Like it or not, legitimacy adds to one's credibility, and that's what will attract and appeal to clients. So, if you live in a city that requires a license to conduct business, consider getting that license. Even if bureaucracy makes your skin crawl.

Now, if you're fortunate to live in a state that doesn't make you pay gross receipts taxes, skip over the next few paragraphs—and know you are a very envied being! Otherwise.........

Let's talk gross receipts. Yes, it is "taxes" and, yes, it is extra work, but it's not anything that anybody can't do, so don't feel intimidated by this. Even if you're not a fan of paying taxes (who the heck is?) look at it like you're doing your civic duty by stimulating your local economy and helping to pay for necessary services. Frankly, we should appreciate paying taxes because that means that we've earned money. And that, my friend, means that we're not an emaciated, homeless, or naked psychic!

I've come across many psychics who considered going pro, but because they were intimidated by the thought of having to do gross receipts taxes, they stayed at their kitchen tables. So, let me take a moment here to explain the whole gross tax thing. First and foremost, it's not so gross because the taxes don't come out of your earnings. It's tax that you'd collect on your consultation fees. See there, that's ouch-less, isn't it?!

To get started, go to your state's taxation and revenue department website. There you should find everything you need to know and do in order to get your business set up to pay gross receipts tax. The site will also provide the guidelines which will help you determine the frequency that you'll pay, which is normally quarterly or monthly. The frequency depends upon your earnings—or what you report that you earn.

Let's look at how it works. Say you charge $50 for a session, and your local tax rate is 5% (if your tax rate is 5%, you're an envied being!). After you complete the session, your client pays you $52.50. The $50 is yours to keep, the $2.50 gets put away until the end of that reporting period. You certainly don't have to put the $2.50 away, but it's less painful that way—meaning that it doesn't feel like it's coming out of your own pocket. When it's due, again, either monthly or quarterly, you follow these simple steps:

1. You log into your account.
2. You plug in your earnings where the form asks for it.
3. You watch as the gross receipts tax you owe is automatically calculated.
4. You pick your payment method and click "Pay."

Voila, done.

The hardest part for a lot of us is keeping track of what we earn. If you use a bookkeeping program or have an actual bookkeeper, it'll be a piece of cake every reporting period. If you use a calendar that hangs on your wall that you write your earnings on, there'll be some added steps to the process. Yep, a calendar is my high-tech system—I did say that anyone could do this!

At this point, you may be wondering why on earth you'd want to put yourself through this ordeal when you can just sit at your kitchen table, do a few readings, and make a few bucks—or get a box of vegetables. Well, the short answer is that you don't have to. But if you want to be a professional psychic, if you want to expand your practice, if you want to make a good living, it'll be worth putting in the time and effort. The first "why on earth" was discussed earlier in this chapter, and that's the legitimacy factor. The second can be explained in just two words: tax deductions! And I'm not just talking about office rent or home office expense. *Oh nooo*, I'm also saying books, CDs, incense, candles, crystals, and any other such profession-related items. As well as classes and seminars—including the travel to and accommodations for those classes and seminars. Hell, even your kitchen table if it truly serves as your primary work space! As long as it directly pertains to your business, it's a legal write-off. By the way, "legal" is a term that your accountant—who's fee is deductible too—would be happy to hear you use. I'm especially emphasizing **LEGAL** if by chance anyone from the IRS happens to be reading this book.

By no stretch of the imagination am I educated in accounting, nor am I claiming to be an expert on taxes—oh lordy, not even close! That's why I highly and unequivocally recommend getting advice from a real tax professional. That person can decisively tell you what can be LEGALLY deducted and what can't. I do know enough to advise you to obtain a receipt for ANY AND ALL expenses you think might be, may be, could possibly be, even remotely possibly be, related to your business! Then let your tax professional be the judge as to which are valid deductions and which aren't.

One more little tidbit: Keep the receipt from the purchase of this book. It's unquestionably related to your business, therefore, it's a write-off! *You are welcome*!!

Next, using your DBA, open a small business checking account. In and of itself, having a separate account lends authenticity to your business in the eyes of Uncle Sam. If your personal account is with a financial institution that doesn't offer free checking to small businesses, don't be shy about looking elsewhere. Great places to look are community banks and credit unions—and don't overlook online banking. Free checking for the little guys can be found, you just have to seek!

Once you have your account set up, make it a point to deposit your earnings into that account and try to pay all your business expenses from there. By doing so, you'll be able to better track your income and expenses, which will make your bookkeeping much easier. Since I'm easily entertained, I appreciate the additional perk to having a business account: you get to use the "commercial accounts only" drive-thru! Try not to look too smug as you breeze past the drivers waiting in the long lines!!

Next, get your business set up to accept debit and credit cards. Nowadays it's as simple as swiping a card on a smartphone. The service can be set up with your bank (but not if your bank is Wells Fargo, whose policy is not to provide credit card services to psychics—I dropped them) or you can use something like Square. There will, of course, be transaction fees, but they're minimal—and they're worth every cent. When your clients have the convenience of using their credit card to pay you, as opposed to only being able to pay you by cash or check, your earnings WILL increase. That's particularly true if you do telephone readings.

I remember *in the old days* when the costs of accepting credit cards was prohibitive, we relied on personal checks and the postal service. If we required prepayment for a reading, we waited for the check to come in before setting up the appointment. Otherwise, we'd have the client send a check afterwards—and would hope that they didn't forget to do so, which was not an uncommon occurrence. I can recall many times when I'd wait a week or two or three, and then would have to make a very awkward call, which typically went something like, *Oh, hi there, I haven't received your check yet. When did you mail it? Oh, you forgot. Yes, thank you, I would appreciate it if you would send it out today.* HATED THAT! But thanks to technology it's now possible to be compensated immediately prior to or post-reading. LOVE THAT!!

It's essential to have business cards printed, or print your own, and heed this: ***always carry them with you.*** Your cards don't have to cost you a fortune or be overly fancy-schmancy. What they do have to be is easily readable. Essentially, their sole purpose is to tell people who you are and how they can reach you. When you hand a potential client a business card, it's not only professional but it's the most personal and one of the most effective ways to advertise. To boot, it's one of the least expensive tools of advertising. Yet, even with all that benefit, it amazes me at how many people don't have business cards, or else, they have them but neglect to carry them. I witnessed that just recently with my best friend, Cindy, when I introduced her to a client of mine. I wanted them to meet because the client was interested in taking one of Cindy's classes. After a great conversation, the client was enthusiastic about taking the class, so she asked Cindy for a business card. After quite a bit of stuttering and stammering, Cindy meekly confessed that she didn't have her cards with her. She was carrying some of my cards, though......hey, thanks, Cindy.

But, oh no, it didn't end there. Since she didn't have a business card to give, she rummaged around in her purse and pulled out a piece of crumpled scrap paper onto which she wrote her name and number, and then handed *that* to her potential student. A unique way of advertising? You could say that. A personal touch? Oh, it sure was. Professional advertising? I'd say not so much. Moral of the story: get some business cards and then ALWAYS carry them with you!

Since you'll always have your business cards in your possession (right?), leave a few wherever you can when you're out and about. Tack your cards up to any and every bulletin board you encounter, such as in grocery stores, coffee shops, book stores, herb stores, or rock shops. Without question, your business cards should be in every metaphysical shop in your area. Wander around town and scatter your cards all over as if they were fairy dust—because you never know where someone will find it. The Universe will orchestrate your card getting into the hands of those who need you. Just get your cards out there. And don't stop at your own town. Leave your cards around even when you visit other cities. If you do phone readings, it doesn't matter where you or they live, so leave your cards behind for people to find. AND, if you happen to be visiting another city, find a metaphysical shop, chat with the owner or staff for a bit, deposit a few of your cards and take one of theirs for your tax records—you just made it a business trip! WRITE-OFF!!

And there's another venue: restaurants with glass bowls! You know the ones that invite you to drop in a business card for a chance to win a free lunch or dinner? Whatever you do, don't pass up that advertising opportunity!! You may not win a meal, but through divine intervention your card can wind up in the hands of someone who needs a psychic. Then again, since divine intervention is already working on your behalf, you might also win that meal!! Wherever a business card is invited, your business card should accept the invitation.

Speaking of invitations, devote sufficient time and effort into setting up your office so that it's a place that feels inviting to your clients. Although I covered the importance of this in a previous chapter, it's worth mentioning again. Regardless of whether it's in your home or in a commercial building, your space should convey a warm and welcoming professionalism. Set it up so that you're completely comfortable working in it, while also keeping the ease of your clientele in mind. That's to say, nothing too extreme.

Also with respect to your space, here's another little tax tidbit: if you use a room in your home and that room is created for and/or dedicated to your work, it would be considered a home office, and, therefore, you should be able to claim home office expense on your taxes. But as I've said before and as I'll say again, check on that with your tax professional.

Launch a website. It doesn't have to be super-elaborate or super-expensive, but some investment should be made in it, because your website introduces you to the world—it's called the worldwide web for a reason. A little fancy-schmancy in this case would serve you well. There's no getting around it, you've gotta have a website. If you want to establish yourself or expand your practice, you've gotta be out there, as in cyberspace, not out in left field, as we're sometimes accused of being! Having a website means people can find you. It's around-the-clock global advertising. Potential clients that view your website can get an idea of who you are, what you do, and get a general feel for you. In addition, having a website bolsters your image as a legitimate business.

It's easier than ever to find someone who can set up a website for you. Of course, the place to start is in your home. Like, if you have a teenager, you've probably found your webmaster! Actually, any kid over toddler age will probably know how to build one!! If not at home, chances are that among your friends you know someone who's computer savvy. You know, the ones we don't talk computers with because they make us feel stupid. You can bet that for three or four nice dinners they'd whip you up a website. They'll still make you feel stupid, but who cares, you'll have your website. However, if you don't want to deal with a computer-geek friend, take inventory of your clientele and you may find a computer graphics professional. If you do, and if you're both agreeable to it, you might trade a few readings. Then again, maybe you know enough to navigate a do-it-yourself site and build your own website. Are you somebody's psychic computer-geek friend? But, if none of the above is a viable option, there are plenty of professionals for hire. Whichever option you go with, yes indeedy, it will be tax-deductible!!

Once you've got your website, connect it with other internet sites. In other words, link and be linked. Include the links on your website to other Lightworkers, such as healers, teachers, other "specialist" psychics, as well as businesses you recommend, like metaphysical, herbal, and gem stores. Then ask those individuals and businesses to add a link to you on their websites. Of course, utilize

Facebook, Linked- In, Twitter, and Instagram, etc. to the absolute max!

If you are so inclined, get yourself out into the "blogosphere." You might begin by commenting on other blogs and engaging in the conversations. Once you've got a following, consider starting your own blog. And, don't forget, whenever and wherever appropriate, mention your own website. It's called marketing, and you've got to do it.

The good news is that marketing ain't what it used to be! Over the last several years, marketing companies, such as Groupon, Living Social, Amazon Local, and the like, have sprung up making it easy and affordable for individuals and small businesses who don't have a lot of advertising capital to reach huge numbers of potential clients. If you're just starting out or you're new to an area, they're great ways to get exposure. If you have the time, the energy, and the fortitude, look into entering into a deal with one of them. A word of warning, though, it's not for the faint of heart.

So, before running a deal, let me give you a few particulars to take into consideration:

- You'll be paid one-quarter of your normal fee. The standard agreement is that the offer you run will be a half-price deal, and then the half-price is split between the marketing company and you. For example, let's say that you normally charge $50 for a half-hour reading and you run a standard deal. That means you'll be offering a half-hour reading for $25. The company will keep $12.50 and you will be paid $12.50, pre-tax.

- One-quarter of your normal fee may not sound like much, and it's not, but if you look at the big picture, you'll see that there's no outlay of cash to advertise, and your service will be introduced to a vast audience, namely, potential clients.

- You will have to pay taxes. The payout checks that the company sends you will be considered income on which you'll have to pay income tax. The marketing company will report to the IRS what they paid you, which means you'd better report to the IRS what you made, as well. If you live in a state where gross receipts tax has to be paid on services, you'll have to pay gross receipts tax on what you earned. For instance, let's say two hundred people purchased your deal at $25, of which you made $12.50 per deal. Now let's say that your city's tax rate is five-percent. That's a tax of sixty-three cents. Multiply that by two hundred and you get $126. If you have to pay gross receipts tax, and because your earnings from these deals are so minimal, I'd suggest you pass the gross receipts tax onto the clients instead of paying it out of your own pocket. It may sound like a petty thing to do, but if you've gotten a good response to your offer, and even if you didn't, that's a substantial chunk of change for you to have to pay.

The issue of gross receipts tax (again, if it's relevant in your state) is that it's not disclosed in big bold letters in the deal, therefore, it's something you'd have to broach with the client. I'd suggest that you inform them of it when they contact you to set up their appointment. Take my advice and don't wait until they get to your office. I actually had a couple of people bristle over paying the few cents because they weren't told in advance—and then they gave me a thumb's down rating because of it!

- Set limits. The first limit is on the amount of deals you sell. I know, I know, that sounds counterintuitive, and you're thinking, *Hell no, the more the better, bring it on*! I'm here to tell you, be careful what you wish to be brought on!!

  It's very exciting when you're watching the tally of purchased vouchers get bigger and bigger. And, honestly, I'm not trying to splash cold water on your excitement here, but in that excitement it's easy to forget that those vouchers will have to be honored. That's where your time, energy, and fortitude will be required—and tested. By setting limits on how many deals you sell, you'll be able to balance your schedule to fit in full-paying clientele. Otherwise, you'll find yourself with a calendar filled up with the deal people.

Next, establish a limit on the length of time your deal runs. You can run a deal anywhere from a few days to a few months. For obvious reasons, the marketing company will push for a long-running deal. Of course, the longer it runs the more deals you'll sell. That's a good thing. Conversely, the longer the deal runs, the longer you're making a fraction of your normal fee because it impinges on the referrals you'll get. Meaning that if you have a long-running deal, like several weeks, anyone who's referred to you will go through the marketing company and buy a deal and won't come to you directly. That's a not so good thing. However, there is a happy medium and it goes something like this: You only run your deal for a short period, a weekend, a week, or whatever feels right to you. After you've done several readings, the referrals from those clients will start calling. For a week or two after the deal expires, you tell the referrals that they missed the deal, BUT, because you're such an *incredibly generous and giving person*, you'll honor the deal price **just for them**.

With that, using the example of a $25 deal, you'll still be working at a cut rate, but it'll be for the full $25, not just $12.50. It's a win-win for you and the client. But, shhhh, don't tell Groupon or Living Social I told you that!

Be sure to make your limits clear to your account representative when you're working out the details of your deal. A limit of any kind is not something they're going to suggest to you.

- Limit yourself. This last part will probably be the hardest. You'll have to be firm with yourself in establishing and then steadfastly holding the limits of your time and energy. When people begin calling to redeem their vouchers, they'll pretty much want their readings immediately, if not sooner—and some of them can get very pushy. For your own sake, you've got to hold your limits. Pace yourself. Otherwise, you will, in no certain terms, burn out really quick.

The two biggest benefits to partnering with one, or all, of these companies are:

- You WILL increase your clientele.
- You WILL get referrals from your newly increased clientele.

Let me offer a couple of final bits of advice about running these offers. First and foremost, try not to have any great expectations about the response you get. Great or small, these three words will determine how many deals you sell: location, location, location! If you live in a pretty progressive area, chances are the response will be sizeable; if you live in, for instance, the bible belt, it may just be minimal. So, if you hit your limit, yay! If you sold just a few deals, yay for what you sold!! Also, don't fool yourself into thinking that each and every person who comes to you through the deal will become a permanent client—even if you gave them an absolutely mind-blowing reading! The fact is, not everyone who walks in your door with their voucher will be a real "seeker." Actually, the only thing some of them will be seeking is a deal! Likewise, you'll get some looky-loos. They're the ones who've been curious about the whole psychic thing and think that it would be a fun thing to do. Then, when you give them their mind-blowing reading, complete with personal information about them that you couldn't possibly know, it scares the piss out of them. With that, as far as they're concerned, it's not fun and you're too freaky, so off they go, never to return—and they're especially not coming back at full price!

The bottom line is this: if it's something that feels right for you to do, use a marketing company as a tool for connecting to a few more clients—keeping in mind that it's a manual tool, not electric, so it requires a lot of elbow grease.

Even for a non-conventional business such as ours, there are conventional ways to expand your business. One way is to check out your local chamber of commerce. Attend a meeting to see if you'd like to become a member—but remember that "location, location, location" will dictate whether you're welcome to join or not. If it's a diverse and welcoming chamber, consider joining to establish yourself in the local business community.

If you're lucky enough to live in a state that has a Holistic Chamber of Commerce, find out where they meet and GO! To see if your city has a branch, go to www.holisticchamber.com. Just like a conventional chamber, they hold monthly meetings, luncheons with speakers, and have other functions for networking, but with the added benefit of being specifically tailored toward the needs and growth of holistic businesses. The *piece de resistance* is that you'd be meeting like-minded folks in a like-minded community—your tribe!!

Any and all small business networking functions are great ways to advertise. But really, any kind of function can be a way to advertise: a wine-tasting event, a friend's barbecue, a bar-mitzvah, a Women's March, etc. Just remember to bring your business cards!

Then there's traditional print advertising. For these venues, I've got to offer up some words of caution. To start with, if you're considering advertising in your local newspapers or periodicals, make sure that their advertising costs are affordable before submitting an ad, because some can be outrageously prohibitive. Of course, you'll also want to make sure that you're not throwing money away. So, before spending a dime, determine whether or not the publication is a good fit for you. To be blunt, I mean that if the publication is blatantly religious and/or conservative, it's probably not going to be a good fit. Also, determine the demographics of its readership before advertising with them. Although an "alternative" newspaper may seem fitting, I can attest from my own experiences, and from the experiences that have been shared with me by other psychics, that you can get—no, rather, you **will** get—some, let's just call them, *very interesting* calls. Therefore, do your research and pick your advertising venues very carefully.

And some advertising venues should be avoided altogether. As in billboard adverting. This is just my opinion, and I admit that I'm being judgmental, but I've seen many billboards advertising psychics and, frankly, I've found them to be categorically tawdry. Typically, they have the psychic dressed in—go ahead, take a guess—that's right, all black. Said psychic is peering intensely outward, telepathically telling the occupants of each passing vehicle that this seer with the big crystal on their head/neck/finger knows EVERYTHING and can solve ALL of the problems for ALL of the people that come to see them. The image feeds the stereotype of "fortune-tellers." And I just think they're creepy. Almost as creepy as billboard advertisements of lawyers.

Frankly, face-to-face is great advertising—but not your face on a billboard. Psychic parties offer that. It's likely that before you became a professional you attended a psychic party yourself, so you know first-hand how much fun they can be. But if you've never been to one, this is how it works: Your friend or client invites several of their friends to their home or office where you would do mini readings for the guests at a discounted price, like a 20/20, twenty minutes for twenty dollars, or whatever you and the host/hostess decide on. The purpose of the party is three-fold:

1. It's for people to be introduced to you and your talent.
2. It's for them get a great reading.
3. It's for you to increase your clientele.

What's more, is that the increase in clientele doesn't stop with the party-goers. Once you've impressed them, those people will certainly tell their friends about you, who will then tell their friends, and on and on it goes. But wait, there's more! Many of the party-goers will offer to host their own parties for you. Just say yes! Accepting those invites will mean different circles of people for you to WOW! So, talk to a few of your current clients about being the host/hostess with the mostest—mostest amazing psychic, that is!!

As a gesture of appreciation, think about throwing in a free reading to your host or hostess. Never underestimate the importance of a thank you gift. It might be an incentive for that client to have another party and invite a totally different group of friends. Most of all, expressing appreciation is just a gosh-darned nice thing to do!

Teaching what you know is another sure way to advertise who you are and what you know. Teaching is a Divine gift, and it's one that provides an opportunity to give as well as to receive. As a teacher, what you give is the depth and breadth of your knowledge; what you receive is the satisfaction of sharing that depth and breadth with others. Yet, it's not about just being altruistic, there's personal gain as well, and that comes when some of your students also become your clients.

Generate even more clients by offering incentives. Perhaps offer a discount to current clients; say, something like ten-percent off their next reading for referring another person to you. Or consider offering a free reading to clients who refer five, ten, or even twenty, other people to you. Doing a few free readings will be worth your time because they'll bring in many more paid ones.

The big events, such as metaphysical faires, draw in the big crowds—and with those events are fantastic opportunities for you to expand your business. Whenever you get an invitation to participate in a big event, if time and energy permit, don't hesitate to accept that invitation. Any opportunity you get to be in an environment where you can meet a lot of people and showcase a bit of what you do is an opportunity that shouldn't be passed up. That's true for anyone, but that's especially true if you're just getting your practice off the ground. And may I remind you once again: bring along lots of business cards!!

Last, but far, far, far from least, never forget that the most powerful form of advertising is word-of-mouth. Keep that in the forefront of your mind, and don't be shy about asking your friends, family, and co-workers to promote you to their friends, family, and co-workers! People will ALWAYS choose to see someone that's been recommended to them over taking a chance on an unknown person they saw advertised on a tawdry and creepy billboard!

One last thing, remember that you're advertising with each and every reading you do. When you give someone a fantastic reading, that advertisement doesn't stop with that one client. They will blast your name out like buckshot—which means that it goes everywhere!

In the business of being psychic, it takes more than just your psychic gift. It also takes some business sense and applying some business strategies. If you're already a professional psychic with a good practice, expand it to the next level. And then to the next, and to the next, and to the next! Make it your business to expand. After all, new clients are trying to find you right now!

CONCLUSION

Let's wax philosophical now, shall we? Do you ever take the time to give any real thought to those age-old questions: *why are we here?* and *what's the meaning of life?* Well, I do. On an unevolved day, the best answer I can come up with is: *beats me.*

But since most of my own waxing is done when I'm in evolved mode, I believe that when we sign up for a lifetime on this planet, the thing at the top of our "to do" list is to make a difference in this world—somewhere, somehow, someway, and for a whole hell of a lot of someones. As spiritual counselors we get to make our difference with each and every life we touch—and that's why we answered the calling to be a professional psychic.

My wish is that this book has made a difference for you. Furthermore, I hope that it helps you to be a more successful and profitable psychic. Then I'll be able to put a big energetic checkmark on my list and say, *Did that*!!

Think of this book as an all-you-can-eat buffet. Feel free to return to these pages again and again to fill up every time you're ready to expand your business to its next level, and the next, and the next.

Above all that, my wish is that you feel all the good juju I'm sending to out you, my amazing colleagues!

Happy Day!

There is no business in this world—or out of this world—like the business of being psychic!!

RECOMMENDED READS

This was perhaps the most challenging part of this book for me. In this chapter, I'm listing some of my all-time favorite books. Unfortunately, there's no way I can list all of the great ones that have enlightened and inspired me, that I consistently refer to, and that I have gleaned so much from. I just can't share as many as I'd like to with you. So, we'll have to settle for my whittled down, can't-do-without, "core" cache that I'd take with me if I was banished to a deserted island. These are the books that I routinely recommend to my clients. Many of these are oldies **and** goodies, which is a testament to their enormous value and timeless wisdom. Since each is a favorite depending on the specific need or circumstance at the moment, I've just listed these gems in alphabetical order.

- *Animal Spirit Guides,* by Steven Farmer
- *Animal-Speak,* by Ted Andrews
- *Ask And It Is Given,* by Abraham-Hicks
- *Bach Flower Therapy,* by Mechthild Scheffer
- *Big Magic,* by Elizabeth Gilbert
- *Broken Open,* by Elizabeth Lesser
- *Co-Dependent No More,* by Melodie Beattie
- *Colors and Numbers,* by Louise Hay
- *Complete Book Of Essential Oils And Aromatherapy,* by Valerie Worwood
- *Conversations With God,* by Neil Donald Walsh
- *Dancing Otters And Clever Coyotes,* by Buffalo Horn Man and Firedancer
- *Destiny Cards Book,* by Robert Camp
- *Dr. Pitcairn's Complete Guide To Natural Health For Dogs And Cats,* by Richard and Susan Pitcairn
- *Excuse Me, Your Life Is Waiting,* by Lynn Grabhorn
- *Feng Shui For Dummies,* Daniel Kennedy and Grandmaster Yun
- *Holographic Universe,* by Michael Talbot
- *How Not To Do A Psychic Reading,* by Viola
- *How To Heal With Color,* by Ted Andrews
- *How To Survive The Loss Of A Love,* by Colgrove, Bloomfield, McWilliams

- *I Wasn't Ready To Say Goodbye,* by Brook Noel and Pamela Blair
- *Law Of Attraction,* by Abraham-Hicks
- *Lightworker's Way,* by Doreen Virtue
- *Nature Of Personal Reality,* by Jane Roberts
- *Permanent Healing,* by Daniel Condron
- *Power Of Now,* by Eckert Tolle
- *Radical Forgiveness,* by Colin Tipping
- *Secrets Of A Millionaire Mind,* by Harv Eker
- *Secrets Of The Lost Mode Of Prayer,* by Greg Braden
- *Seth Speaks,* by Jane Roberts
- *Simple Abundance,* by Sarah Ban Breathnach
- *Sun Signs,* by Linda Goodman
- *The Seth Material,* by Jane Roberts
- *The Vortex,* by Abraham-Hicks
- *Top Ten Things Dead People Want To Tell You,* by Mike Dooley
- *Women's Bodies, Women's Wisdom,* by Dr. Christiane Northrup
- *You Can Heal Your Life,* by Louise Hay
- *Your Soul's Plan,* by Robert Swartz

Also, some fun fiction, with an added bonus of wisdom:

Breakfast With Buddha, Lunch With Buddha, and *Dinner With Buddha,* by Roland Merullo. And if you're interested in a little (a lot, actually) sacrilegious, laugh-out-loud amusement, I highly recommend *Lamb,* by Christopher Moore. However, if blasphemy is definitely not your thing, forget I ever mentioned this book.

Enjoy!

Made in the USA
Columbia, SC
28 November 2018